CRACKING IIT-JEE

CRACKING IIT-JEE

I Dream of Studying at an IIT

Subhash Jain

Ocean Books Pvt. Ltd.
ISO 9001:2015 Publishers

Published by
Ocean Books (P) Ltd.
4/19 Asaf Ali Road,
New Delhi-110 002 (INDIA)
e-mail: info@oceanbooks.in

ISBN 81-8430-064-6
CRACKING IIT-JEE
by Shri Subhash Jain

Edition
2025

Price
₹ 400.00 (Rupees Four Hundred Only)

Printed at
Narula Printers, Delhi

Tribute

There was a time when I thought
God walked beside you,
But now I see God moves
With every step you take.
There was a time when I thought
God loved you,
But now I feel you are the love
I often speak of.
There was a time when I thought
God has blessed you,
But now I know
You are His blessing to me.

"I dedicate this book, with deep respect and great love, to my parents. "

Contents

Cracking IIT-JEE:

"Consciously choosing to go as far as I can with all that I have."

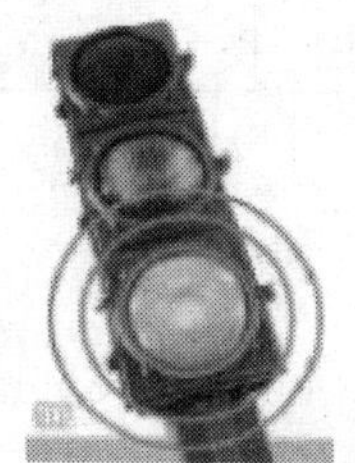

I	First Words	9
II	Introduction	13
1	Mission IITJEE	17
2	The Nature of Strengths	22
3	An IITian	29
4	Brain Game	34
5	Design Career	44
6	Time Management	51
7	Winning Wave	59
8	Master Move	65
9	Right Time	71
10	Inner Voice	79
11	Fast Memorize	87
12	Probe Physics	93

13	Create Chemistry	102
14	Measure Mathematics	108
15	Paper Tactics	115
16	JEE Psychoanalysis	123
17	Exam Anxiety	132
18	JEE Count Down	140
19	Introduction IIT	147
20	Quest Questions	153

I

First Words

Thanks to Man of Mars, Woman of Venus, Children of Heaven and All Gods and Goddesses of Universe.

I have been blessed to have an unexpected support squad of friends, family, and colleagues who have helped me on every pace of the personal voyage I call a life. These people deserve deep thanks and genuine admiration. So I express all my appreciation to each and every one of them for assisting me as I walk the path of my personal mission. Sometimes words don't adequately convey the depth of our gratitude to the many individuals involved in the development of this tome, yet without making acknowledgments the message would go unrecorded.

I express my respect, love and gratitude to my mother and to my father Late Mr. M C Jain. I feel a deep sense of gratitude to my wife and my sons for supporting my many travels and involvement inside and outside the home.

"Only those return to Eternity
Who on the earth seek out Eternity."

O ye who do believe, seek aid from patience and from prayer, verily, God is with the patient.

"Turn Thy Face towards the Sacred Mosque" No Human soul but hath a guardian over it.

Allah, as taught to **Muhammad - Quran**

In October 1959, the United States felt deeply humiliated by the launching of the Soviet spaceship **Sputink**. American scientists had been working on launching an American spacecraft for a number of years. Then U S president John F. Kennedy said, ***"We choose to go to the Moon."***

On July 20, 1969, Apollo 11's Lunar Module approached the moon's surface with American astronauts Neil Armstrong and Edwin "Buzz" Aldrin.

"That's one small step for man, one giant leap for mankind."

—Neil Armstrong

*"... We need to dare, to dare again, always to **DARE**."*

In the name of **God, GO AHEAD!**

II
Introduction

"The future is beyond knowing, but the present is beyond belief. We make so much noise with technology that we cannot discover that the star gate is in our foreheads. But the time has come; the revelation has already occurred, and the guardian seers have seen the lightning strike the darkness we call reality. And now we sleep in the brief interval between the lightning and the thunder."

What does it take to crack IITJEE?

Cracking IITJEE is nuance and complex, not to mention brutally hard. As Archimedes declared, "the key to all building is leverage." If you have been struck in your career or personal life, working harder will probably not get you what you want, but working smart will.

Are you ready to take a unique trip to the shores of success, tides of IITJEE preparation and the land of fulfillment?

Have you ever thought about your thinking and how you know? On a very simplified level, you could say that every thing you know came to you through your senses. You see, hear, taste and touch things of your choosing and you can also smell things in your surroundings. Information is gathered and sent to your brain by your sense organs.

Somehow, your brain processes all this information in an attempt to find order and make sense of it all. You neither thrive in your life just by reading a book, nor can satisfy your appetite by reading a cookbook. **IITJEE** is an adventure to be fully experienced, experimented with, and committed to. A book is a poor substitute for experiencing what the adventure has to offer. But a good guidebook can help it and help to illuminate your experiment.

We had one goal in writing "Cracking IITJEE" to create the most vital book you've ever owned.

Finding order helps you understand the world and what may be happening at a particular place and time. Finding order also helps you predict what may happen next, which can be very important in a lot of situations. New ideas, practical tools and study strategies are essential to attain not only success in IITJEE, but also a good rank.

One of the biggest misconceptions about studying is the big mystery about how to do it. Another misconception is that some people are just naturally better at it than others. They seem to have been born with a gift that makes learning come easy for them. Each one of us is a thinker, philosopher, explorer, learner and teacher, in one's own small way, learning from the ages.

A true scientist is nurtured from the school up-wards to scientific establishments. We teach our scientists to make a lot of mistakes we call them experiments and that those mistakes would turn into positive things. Go ahead and attempt new things and you will learn from it. Only, if there are inspired and dedicated school science teachers in abundance, there will be sufficient number of inspired students who would like to take science as a career option and who may one day become a successful scientist or technocrat.

I was wrong! For nearly half of my professional career, I was wrong about how to help aspirants to achieve. I had the wrong focus, made inaccurate assumptions, used faulty logic, and come to the wrong conclusion about how to increase aspirants' achievement. I was using the wrong approach. About the only thing I did right during those early years was to invest myself in students, express my care and concern for them as people, and encourages them.

But I began to see potential problems with my assumptions.

- Many aspirants do not do the expected level of preparation.
- The whole issue of preparation is complex, because there are many types of preparation that the aspirants require in order to achieve the goal.

After interviewing hundreds of successful candidates, I came to believe that the types of preparation aspirants needed included three broad areas: competitive skills, background knowledge, and self-management skills. This book has been written from a lifetime of experience and diligent observations in the hope that it may help aspirants in all parts of the IITJEE preparation.

It has been well said that "Life is a tough school because the exams come first and the learning afterwards", this book is a small attempt to provide some learning before the exams arrive.

And when you get into IIT and people ask you how you succeeded, make sure you drop me a line on *subhashedu@yahoo.co.in*; I would love to read from you or to hear on 098710 32142. May this book serve as your lighthouse, compass and map on your journey to the **IITJEE**.

Read, learn, enjoy and apply what you study.

God bless!

"One good idea applied immediately is better than five ideas memorized and stored unused in the mind."

1

Mission IITJEE

THE ROAD AHEAD

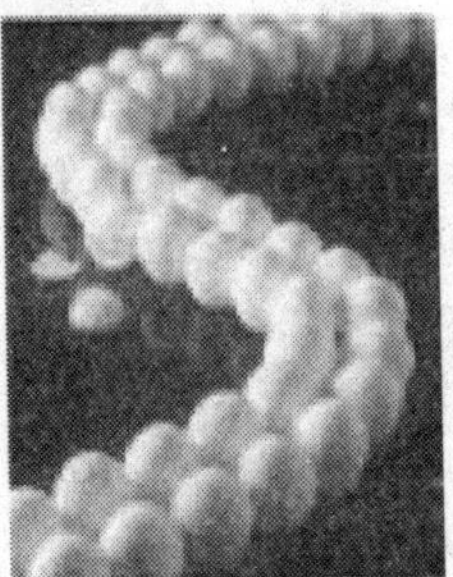

"Champions Everywhere - Passion a must"

Aspirants of IITJEE undertake hazardous journey, small chances, bitter fight, and constant study, honour and recognition in case of success. In the adventures of Alice in wonderland, Alice came up to the caterpillar and asked him which road she should take. He asked her where she was going. She replied that she didn't know. He said, "Then it doesn't matter what road you take."

Make a road map for your work, so you know how to get from where you are now to where you want to be in the future. With objectives and goals, it becomes clear what you need to do, and you can get it done!

It is important to remember that science-oriented students are not all alike; any more than all artists or all politicians are alike.

Your success will depend on going where your particular interests lead you. Most doctors' professional lives are filled with caring for people and continuously learning about the human body. People study social science because they want to understand more about issues and problems of everyday life. They want to become better equipped to engage in discussion, to provide an informed view or to be more active citizens.

It essentially requires an adequate understanding of oneself in terms of academic potentials, attributes, talents, interests, personality, values, expectations and resources. When you are choosing a career, you have to consider what you expect from your job power, money, status, discipline, command or challenge. Interest in the job is absolutely vital for growth in any profession. In choosing a career it is important that you know yourself well, what you want from your profession and also what the world of occupation has to offer.

The first, called **"Underneath It All,"** is conceptual. The strong mission and concrete values are absolute necessity of aspirant.

IITJEE cracking is about managing the arc and the quality of your specialized study. There is a central quality, which is the root criterion of IITJEE and spirit in an aspirant. This quality is objective and precise, but it cannot be named.

"Innovating regularly", at all levels, in all subjects, is the second basis for sustainable strategy. The real world of innovating is serendipitous and passion-filled. So – I plead you to sit back and kick up your feet on the table before delving into it.

As is often the case, where there's smoke, there is fire. Where there is a ***Will*** there is a way.

INDIAN TREND

Eight Indian American high school seniors are among 40 high school seniors named finalists in prestigious Intel Science Talent Search 2008. The competition, often called Junior Nobel Prize, is America's oldest and most prestigious high school competition.

Between 1990 and 2000, the Indian population in the US grew 113% - 10 times the national average of 13%. Indians own 50% of all economy lodges and 35% of all hotels in the US, which have a combined market value of almost $40 billion. One in every nine Indians in the US is a millionaire, comprising 10% of US millionaires.

A University of California, Berkeley study reported that one-third of the engineers in Silicon Valley are of Indian descent, while 7% of valley's hi-tech firms are led by Indian CEOs.

Indians have the highest educational qualifications of all ethnic groups in the US. Almost 67% of all Indians have a bachelor's or higher degree (compared to 28% national). Almost 40% of all Indians have a master's, doctorate or other professional degree, which is five times the national average.

To be a Superman, all you need is to discover, activate, conquer and enjoy.

DISCOVER

- Your destiny and passion
- Wholeness, body, soul and spirit
- The uniqueness in the people around you

CONQUER

- Programs that short circuit your dreams
- Hindering fears that sabotage success
- Fears and misconceptions that hinder you

ACTIVATE

- The gifts and abilities that God gave you
- Favourable relationships
- Success and destiny

ENJOY

- A fulfilling an purposeful future
- Feeling and being whole, Body, Soul & Spirit
- Life!

Every year, India's top aspirants appear in JEE of the IIT's to compete against one another in the most dramatic of contests. For each aspirant years of training and mental preparation must be timed to deliver a peak performance at the right moment.

Over the years of competition, the exams have created an unforgettable gallery of technocrats men and women. If you advance confidently in the direction of your dreams, and endeavours to live the life, which you have imagined, you will meet with an unexpected success in common hours. If you aspire to the highest place, it is no disgrace to stop at the second, or even the third place. Since, Twenty years from now, you will be more disappointed; by the things you didn't do, than by the ones you did. So throw off the bowlines, sail away from the safe harbour; catch the trade winds in your sails.

BRAINWAVE: *There in not a thought is being thought in the West or the East that is not active in some Indian mind.*

KEEP IN MIND: *Oh aspirant be wise. There exists no other world but this. That is certain.*

THINK ZONE: ***Every day, there is a new question.***

2

The Nature of Strengths

The strength is the ability to provide consistent, near perfect performance in a given activity. But strength begins with a talent, so let's start there. A talent is a naturally recurring pattern of thought, feeling, or behavior that can be productively applied.

Talents are like 'diamonds in the rough,' whereas strengths are like diamonds that show brilliance after they have been carefully cut and polished. Just as finished diamonds start as diamonds in the rough, strengths start as talents. And just as rough diamonds are naturally found in the earth, talents are naturally found within you. But while diamonds are refined with blades and polishing wheels, strengths are produced when talents are refined with *knowledge* and *skill.*

A great number of talents naturally exist within you, and each of them is very specific. Your specific set of talents is a major part of what makes you a unique person, and that uniqueness holds great value for you and those around you. And your talents work in various combinations each time you do something very well, in your own unique way. This combination of talents and strengths makes each person like no other. While each person defines success for himself, achievement and excellence result from fully developing and applying strengths.

There is a direct connection between your talents and your achievements. Your talents empower you. They make it possible for you to move to higher levels of excellence and fulfill your potential. This is why it is so important for you to know, understand, and value your talents. And not only do talents help you do something well once; they help you do it well over again. The great value of talent is not that it help you achieve, but in achieving with excellence. Your greatest talents are inextricably linked to your top achievements and to what you do best.

Talents are like muscles. If you use them, will help you achieve. Further, if you develop them, they will become stronger and even more capable of helping you achieve. Your talents make you exceptional. Therefore, coming to know, understand, and value your talents is directly linked to achieving in classes, careers, and throughout your life.

Unlike talent, which must naturally exist within you, skills and knowledge can be acquired. Skills are the ability to perform the specific steps of an activity. Knowledge consists of facts and lessons learned.

IITJEE ASPIRANT STRENGTHS QUEST

My education is very important to me, so I have to

devote a lot of time to my classes. "I'm going to earn an A in every class and I'm going to ask my teachers for opportunities to earn extra credit so I can turn that A into an A+.

General Academic Life

If you are in school, consider it your academic career. Do everything you can to be a person of excellence now. It is your best preparation for future excellence. Ask each of your teachers to clarify their expectations for your performance.

The seeds of your personal greatness your talents are already in you. Therefore, your strengths quest your quests to achieve excellence and become all you can be through your own natural talents are really a quest to discover, develop, and apply who you truly are.

Your strengths quest is a lifelong adventure. Each of the three aspects discovery, development, and application will continue throughout your life.

Gaining Direction for Quest

Your awareness, development, and application of your strengths are inextricably linked to your motivation level. To the extent that you fully involve yourself in a strengths quest, your motivation will increase, and that will revolutionize your life.

Achiever describes a constant need for achievement. You feel as if every day starts at zero. By the end of the day you must achieve something tangible in order to feel good about yourself. And by 'every day' you mean every single day workdays, weekends, and vacations. No matter how much may feel you deserve a day of rest, if the day passes without some form of achievement, no matter how small, you will feel dissatisfied. You have an internal fire burning inside you. It pushes you to do more, to achieve more. After each accomplishment is reached, the fire dwindles for a moment, but very soon it rekindles itself, forcing you toward the next accomplishment.

Ideas Turn into Action

Action is the best device for learning. You make a decision, you take action, you look at the result, and you learn. How can you grow if you have nothing to react to? Well, you believe you can't. You must put yourself out there. The bottom line is this: You know you will be judged not by what you say, not by what you think, but by what you get done. This does not frighten you. It pleases you.

You can see how ideas can be turned into action. You want to do things now, rather than simply talk about doing during them. Activator talents are valuable, they generate the energy to get things going and then done. This theme brings innovation and creative approaches to problem solving.

Go with the flow you can move ahead, you can deal with everything from simple to complex problems and still find a way to make progress. You enjoy coordinating the entire complex factor that go into making a project successful.

Analytical Approach

The philosopher Friedrich Nietzsche was quoted as saying, "He who has a 'why' to live for can bear almost any 'how.'"

You peel the layers back until, gradually, the root causes are revealed. Others see you as logical and rigorous. "When I saw a kid, I took a clock apart just to see how it worked. When I was the gears and how they worked together, it made perfect sense. I was able put it back together very quickly."

You search for the reason why things are they are.

Analytical talents are valuable because they enable you to big deep, find the root causes and effects, and then develop clear thoughts about what is true. This type of thinking helps you become clearer about what excellence is and how it can be attained.

Competitive Attitude

Competition is rooted in comparison. When you look at the world, you are instinctively aware of other people's performance. Like all competitors, you need other people. You need to compare. If you can compare, you can compete, and if you can compete, you can win. And when you win, there is no feeling quite like it. You like other competitors because they invigorate you. You like contests because they must produce a winner. You particularly like contests where you know you have the inside track to be the winner. Although you are gracious to your fellow competitors and even stoic in defeat, you don't compete for the fun of competing. You compete to win.

The power of perspective

What is the big 'why' of your life? What are you ultimately trying to get done? What mission, purpose, or ultimate objective do you want to accomplish.

These are the questions of 'mission'. Once you have formulated and clarified your personal mission. Connecting your talents and mission is critical because your mission motivates you to develop your talents into strengths, and your strengths will empower you fulfill your mission.

Attitude ⟹ Performance ⟹ Skill

STRENGTHS AND CAREER PLANING

Mark Twain told the story of a man who searched his whole life for the world's greatest general. When the man died, he arrived in heaven and walked up to St. Peter and said, "I'm looking for the world's greatest general."

St. Peter replied, "I know. We've been expecting you, and I have good dews. If you will look right over there, you will see the world's greatest general."

The older man excitedly looked over and said, "That's not the world's greatest general. That man was a cobbler on Main Street in my hometown."

St. Peter responded, but had he been a general, he would have been the greatest general ever."

This story is not meant to demean cobbler at all. The work of a cobbler is meaningful and requires very special talents. But the story does raise some fundamental questions: Did the cobbler know what he had the potential to do? Did he know that he had the talent to be the world's greatest general? Did any body try to convince him that he could be destined for greatness?

Twain's tale hints at a painful truth: There are plenty of perfectly good cobbers out there who could have been great generals, given the opportunity or encouragement. Maybe, given the choice, they would still have chosen to be cobbers. But they also could have purposed completely different, perhaps historic, careers. Give this tale some thought when planning your own career.

You are not alone who is struggling with career planning. The process of career planning is a challenge for everyone. Target your values before you target a career. Begin your career today and live accordingly. You won't rest until you reach your most highly desired goals – and they must be your goals.

BRAINWAVE: *If you want to make God laugh, tell him your future plans.*

KEEP IN MIND: *Sometimes the path you're on is not as important as the direction you're heading.*

THINK ZONE: *Explore! Dream! Discover!*

3

An IITian

An IITian:

- Has a good education
- Makes a difference
- Is liked and admired
- Has job security with high remuneration
- Enjoys good personal and professional relationships
- Meets goals

The power of our attainment is directly proportional to the levels of our sacrifice in life. Every worthwhile accomplishment has a price tag attached to it. The question is always whether you are willing to pay the price to attain it – in hard work, sacrifice, patience, trust and staying power.

To be an IITian you should have

- Strong Will and Vitality

- Discipline and Constancy
- Objectivity and Practicality

A key ingredient in achieving what you want what you have understood and how your energy affects your performance. Let us explore how the secrets of your power centers can give you a valuable edge:

Power center	Location	Function
Crown	Top of head	Intuition and Inspiration
Forehead	Center of forehead	Memory and imagination
Mid-bow	Between eyebrows	Discipline and constancy
Throat	Middle of throat	Objectivity and practicality

RECOGNIZING THE UNEXPECTED

Albert Einstein (1954) wrote: It is in fact nothing short of a miracle that the modern methods of instruction have not yet entirely the holy curiosity of inquiry... It is a very grave mistake think that the enjoyment of seeing and searching can be promoted by means of correction and a sense of duty.

Charles Good year had been working for several years on how to preserve and cure raw rubber so it would maintain its elastic characteristics regardless of temperature. His development of vulcanization, the method used to process rubber for tyres; occurred by following an instinct he said had come to him in a dream: Combine sulfur with the rubber. He wrote: I was encouraged in my efforts by the reflection that what is hidden and unknown, and cannot be discovered by scientific research, will most likely be discovered by accident, if at all, and by the man who applies himself most perseveringly to the subject, and is most observing of everything selected thereto.

Samuel Morse conceived the telegraph after a chance conversation about electricity with a fellow passenger aboard a steamship returning to the United States.

The telephone was developed from an accidental occurrence. Alexander Graham Bell and his associate, Thomas Watson, were experimenting with the possibility that a vibrating membrane might be made to produce changes in electric current similar to the way the tiny human eardrum transmits vibration to the hammer, anvil, and stirrup, the tiny sound-conduct-transmitting bones in the inner part of the apparatus while Bell was in another room listening at the receiving end Suddenly Bell heard a twang over the receiver. One of the springs in the transmitter had become stuck, and Watson had caused it to twang while trying to get it free, generating a small electric current that was transmitted along the wire to the receiver. This accident ultimately resulted in the development of the telephone.

The production of penicillin can be traced to be a chance observation by Sir Alexander Fleming in 1928 that some airborne material, alter shown to be mold, had contaminated Petri dishes of culture medium on which colonies of staphylococcus bacteria were rowing, killing the bacteria. Fleming did not understand the medical implications of this discovery, and several years later, Gladys Hobby, together with Martin Henry and Karl Meyer, perfected penicillin and became the first to cure a patient with drug. Hobby subsequently developed Terramycin, a more powerful antibiotic.

In each of these cases, the discovery was made because people were able to recognize the significance of something they had never seen before! This is one of the primary characteristics of scientist, new knowledge is not produced simply by committing old knowledge to memory, though certainly some prior knowledge is necessary as a foundation, new knowledge is produced by being able to observe what others have not observed, ask questions no one has thought to ask try things no one has thought to try, make inferences no one has thought to make, sort things in ways no one has sorted them, and focus less on right answer and more on sensible answers. New knowledge is produced as the result of being able science.

☑ DON'T GIVE CHANCE TO STEAL YOUR DREAMS

There was a hunter who came into the possession of a special bird dog. The dog was the only one of its kind, because it can walk on water. One day he invited a friend to go hunting with him so that he could show off his prized possession. After some time, they shot a few ducks, which fell into the river. The man ordered his dog to run and fetch the birds. The dog ran on water to fetch the birds. The man was expecting a compliment about the amazing dog, but did not receive it. Being curious, he asked his friend if the friend had noticed anything unusual about the dog. The friend replied, "Yes, I did see something unusual about your dog. Your dog can't swim!"

More than 90% of the people that we face everyday are negative. They choose to look at the hole in the middle rather than the doughnut. Do not expect compliments or encouragement from them. These are the people who cannot pull you out of your present situation. They can only push you down. So be aware of them, spend less time with them, and do not let them steal your dreams away from you.

"To be nobody but yourself on the earth that is trying it's best day and night to make you like everybody else is to fight the hardest battle any human being will fight and keep on fighting."

There is no man in this world without some manner of tribulation or anguish, though he is a king or a pope. When we devote ourselves to the strict and unsparing performance of duty, the result comes of its. Life has no smooth road for any of us; and in the stimulating atmosphere of a high aim the very roughness stimulates the climber to steadies steps till the legend, 'over steep ways to the stars', fulfills self. How we feel about ourselves is more important than how others feel about us; the survival of the fittest is the age less law of nature, but the fittest are rarely the strong. The fittest are those endowed with the qualifications for adaptation, the ability to accept the inevitable and conform to the unavoidable, to harmonize with changing conditions.

BRAINWAVE: *"... always aim at perfection and be satisfied only with excellence."*

KEEP IN MIND: *Success is falling nine times and getting up ten. When it is dark enough, you can see the stars.*

THINK ZONE: Worry about the chances you miss when you *don't even try.*

4

Brain Game

EVERY BRAIN IN THE GAME

Helping you thrive in that playground is one of the important elements of play to win! It makes a difference whether we consider ourselves pawns in a game whose rules we call 'reality' or as players in a game who know that the rules are 'real' only to the extent that we have created or accepted them. A set of rules specifying the goal of the game and the roles of the participants, including the permissible actions of, and information available to, each participant, the criteria for establishing progress, the criteria for termination of the game, and the distribution of payoffs. Finally, the rules specify why the game is being played.

IITJEE: A different endeavour in which the outcome is tough, but the possibility of great reward exists.

The Times Higher Education Supplement ranking of international universities:

1 BERKELEY

2 MIT

3 IIT: THE PRIDE OF NATION

It's not a secret that the IIT: Indian Institute of Technology is India's best-known education brand in the world. This year IITs got global recognition from an international panel of academics for the strength and rigour of their academic programme. The rankings developed by The Times Higher Education Supplement (THES) in London ranks the seven IITs above other leading global tech institutions like Stanford and Georgia Tech University in the peer score ranking of technology universities. In fact, IITs are the third, after MIT and University of California, Berkeley; the rankings are based on peer review of 2,375 academics, who are involved in research, in areas like science and technology, biomedicine and humanities. THES describes the IITs as 'a source of Indian national pride as well as innovation and wealth'. MIT had the greatest faculty; each one is as capable, active and caring as amazing role models. With 20 Nobel Prize winners from its faculty and 24 from its alumni and a history spanning more than 150 years, the University of California, Berkeley is one of the world's great institutions of higher education.

What is great about IIT? High achievers from different parts of the country, different social backgrounds indeed the cream of the country, which is extracted by JEE. Ratio of selection 100 to 1 whereas In MIT 10 to 1.

IIT's one former Director says, "I am really quite sad that we as teachers are not doing our job properly why do we say 'among the world's best five' and not 'the world best"?

The IIT environment is very conducive to growth; scholars have a rich life, both curricular and extra curricular. Living in the IIT hostel is a great growing experience, every one at IIT is bright and they learn a lot from one another. Even IIT alumni's excellent performance opened the doors wide for next generations of IIT graduates.

Over the years many have voiced concerns about 'Brain Drain' about the leakage of IITian into not only in non-technical professions but also to foreign countries hence the consequent loss of technically trained manpower to the nation. In democracy no one can force a career choice on anyone. Most parents ignore the fact that children those are good in the science and mathematics may also be good in others such as languages, history, philosophy, music, swimming, designing etc. At the school leaving age, they are not aware of their natural inclinations; only we push them into what is currently in vogue.

India's first Prime Minister Jawarhar Lal Nehru dreamt of many institutions to build India. The IIT was one such dream, which has turned out to be a jewel in the crown of independent India...the IIT is now a world brand on which country proud. IIT has been producing technocrats, scientists, and managers. Among them some are most prominent executives, presidents, entrepreneurs and CEO of organisations.

IIT-JEE: One of the toughest exams to crack, flattering stiffer every year!

Year	JEE Aspirants Approximately
1960	20,000
1970	40,000
1980	<1,00,000

1990	~1,00,000
2000	>1.00,000
2005	2,00,000
2006	<3,00,000
2007	~3,00,000
2008	>3,00,000

Let numbers do the speaking. All the six are from different states of the top 10 who cracked IIT-JEE this year were coached at Kota. And if you look at the overall figure, more than 3,500 of the 7,800 students who got through to IIT-JEE were associated with the numerous coaching institutes that have sprung up in this small town in Rajasthan. Again, consider the figures.

Some 3.2 lakh students took IIT-JEE this year. Only 7,800 qualified. That's a success rate of just over 1%. Now, 25,000 students took the help of Kota institutes and over 3,500 qualified. That's a strike rate of 14%. Last year, only four of the top 10 in IIT-JEE were from Kota. It is also interesting to note that almost 50% of those qualified JEE were just from 5 cities: Delhi, Hyderabad, Jaipur, Kota and Kanpur.

BLUE PRINT OF A TECHNOCRAT

Every one is a unique combination of different characteristics determined by gender, body type, temperament, personality, intelligence, and style of learning. Every one regardless of gender has his or her one's unique balance of male and female characteristics. Within the developing mind, heart, and body of every child is the perfect blueprint for that child's development. All are born with tremendous enthusiasm.

ADOLESCENCE (9-21): Develops Own Identity vs. Role Confusion

Early Adolescence	Middle Adolescence	Late Adolescence
	Decisions Making	21 **EARLY ADULT TRANSITION** 18
	18 **TEEN TRANSITION** 12	Self Esteem
12 **PRE TEEN TRANSITION** 9	Skill Development	

CHILDHOOD (0-9): Observes vs. Adaptability

Early Childhood	Middle Childhood	Late Childhood
	Expand their own world	9 **LATE CHILDHOOD TRANSITION** 6
	6 **CHILDHOOD TRANSITION** 3	Explore the world
3 **EARLY CHILDHOOD TRANSITION** 0	Adapt the surroundings	

BE MINDFUL NOT MINDLESS

Every generation is different from the previous one. Today teens are more sensitive than any previous generation. Besides being unique and different, each comes into this world with his / her own bundle of issues and problems. No one is perfect. What you see in your mind is what you create; what you think about is what you get; and what you speak is what you become. You can maintain a high-quality mental outlook that rejects the thoughts and the language that hold you back.

Mental preparation is essential to any competitive event: coaches continually urge players to 'think!' or to 'concentrate!' Games are said to have been won as a result of mental preparation or lost for the lack of it. Your brain is a 'thought factory'; production in your thought factory is under the charge of two foremen:

I.  **Mr. Mindful** - is in charge of manufacturing positive thoughts; specializes in producing reasons why you can, why you're qualified, why you will. Replace the phrase "I will." "I'll try" means "I feel compelled to do it, but I really don't like to do it." A try is nothing more than that.

II.  **Mr. Mindless** - produces negative, depreciating thoughts; expert in developing reasons why you can't, why you're weak, why you're inadequate and "why you will fail". A person is a product of his own thoughts. Be extra, extra cautious about negators – they destroy your plan to think yourself to success.

Think positively - change your thoughts and you change your world. Be Mindful and create ***success***. Believe, really believe, you can move a mountain and you can. Not many people believe that they can move mountains. So, as a result, not many people do. Those who believe they can move mountains, they do. Those who believe they can't, they cannot.

Belief triggers the power to do. It is not possible to win high-level success without meeting opposition, hardship and setback. But it is possible to use setbacks to propel you forward. Belief is the thermostat that regulates what we accomplish in life. Belief, the "I'm-positive-I-can" attitude generates the power, skill, and energy needed to do. When you believe I can-do-it, the how-to-do-it develops.

Every artist dips his brush into his own soul, and paints his own nature into his picture as he does in living his life.

☑ YOU'VE MORE BRAIN THAN YOU THINK

Tell me, and I will forget.
Show me, and I will remember.
Involve me, and I will understand.

—Confucius

There is no limit to what you can imagine, and with commitment, with effort, what you can imagine you can become. Put your mind to work for you, believe that you can do it. The world will tell you that you can't. Yet, in your belief you will find the strength; you'll find the ability to do it anyway. One's mind, once stretched by a new idea, never regains its original dimension. I am a great believer in luck, and I find that the harder I work, the more I have of it as, "Luck chooses those who work for it." When scientists learn how to use their imagination, not only visualization, great discoveries will result in the unthinkable! When three minds meet and cooperate: the concrete mind of the scientists, the creative imagination of the artists and the guiding principles of the philosopher, the future world will be a super-world.

You are today where your thoughts have brought you. You will be tomorrow where your thoughts have taken you. Power, talents and abilities lie dormant within us. Bear in mind that because you haven't done a certain thing up-to the present that is no reason why you should not do it in the future. Men are failures not because they are stupid, but because they are not sufficiently impassioned. Failure is not falling down. It is remaining there when you have fallen. Have confidence in yourself. With confidence, battles have been won; inventors have seen their dreams come true: and puny weaklings have grown to giant stature. Only because they believed in themselves, one of the important factors in developing intelligence is observation. Through observation you see things minutely and attentively.

Have not many people seen an apple fall to the ground? But it took Isaac Newton to observe it and discover the law of gravity. Alexander Bell also observed and discovered the telephone. To the observant Albert Einstein goes the honour of discovering the principles of relativity and to Thomas Edison idea of electric bulb. Be observant; keep your mind open all the time, watch how things are done especially by more experienced people than yourself.

Look out for details. Be sure that you have a full knowledge of what you are expected to do and you will avoid the mistake of the workmen who were discovered by an executive tearing down the wall and door of his office. Don't expect an angel to come down from heaven and provide you with a plainly marked road map, indicating with large arrows when, where and how you could develop yourself that's your business. Failure to use your talent is to hurt yourself.

The great artist Leonard De Vinci out it well when he said, "Iron rusts from disuse, stagnant water loses its purity and in cold weather becomes frozen, even so does infection sap the vigorous of the mind. A mind that is alert, interested and eager is a golden key both to health and to the enjoyment of life." Every person has infinite capabilities; the only difference between a wizard and an ordinary person is that the wizard uses more of his or her latent capabilities—and works harder.

The playing to win epitaph:	**The playing not to lose epitaph:**
I took the risk.	I survived.
I discovered who I was.	I didn't get hurt.
I changed.	I was comfortable.
I grew.	I never lost.
I learned.	I was always right.
I was an adventurer.	I really knew who I was.

BE REALISTIC

"When I was growing up, my parents wanted me to be a doctor like my father. The moment I came out of my mother's

womb, they thought I had a stethoscope around my neck. But I never wanted to be a doctor. When I was fifteen, I broke the news to my parents that I didn't want to take up Biology, world war III started. I said if you make me do it, I will fail. They talked me into studying Physics, Chemistry and Biology. I did Zero work, I fared poorly in Biology, and got an 'A' for Physics and Chemistry. I remember, I wrote my name on the Biology paper and fell asleep. After that my parent realized they couldn't force me to do anything I didn't want to do. Later on I took Math and appeared in JEE and became an IITIAN."

We decide our own fate by our actions. It is not a matter of sitting back and accepting. You have to gain mastery over yourself.

BRAINWAVE: *Both optimists and pessimists contribute to our society. The optimist invents the aeroplane and the pessimist the parachute.*

KEEP IN MIND: *Crises and deadlocks, when they occur have at least this advantage: They force us to think.*

THINK ZONE: *I rant therefore I am.*

5

Design Career

YOU AND SCIENCE

What we know today as science was originally called philosophy. The word philosophy was coined during the time of Aristotle from words, philos (love) and sophia (wisdom). Thus, the term philosophy literally means 'love of wisdom'. The term science comes from the Latin word scientia (to know). 'A possession of knowledge' A branch of knowledge or study dealing with a body of facts or truths systematically arranged and showing the operation of general laws; skill; proficiency.'

Science is the system of knowledge, founded on formal axioms or theories constructed from observation and experiment. Science such as physics and chemistry, which try to describe and account for natural phenomena, are often studied by theories, which express mathematically a principle underlying numerous observations. Ideally, such theories encompass all previous knowledge on the phenomena and can be used to make testable predictions; they are discarded or at a variance with experimental evidence.

The prosperity of a country in the world of today lays how a country uses the knowledge of science at its disposal and what its scientists do. To make scientists, just learning science is not enough. It is to learn to make a science that makes scientist. Students should learn science the way science is done. Chemistry should be learned the way chemists practice their profession; physics should be learned the way physics explore the reached world; biology should be learned the way biologists examine life processes.

CAREERS IN SCIENCE AND ENGINEERING

People seek careers in science or engineering for many reasons. Some have specific goals: they wish to cure diseases or combat hunger or reduce pollution; or they dream of developing the next laser, transistor, or vehicle for space travel; or they imagine building companies that capitalize on new engineering capabilities. Some choose careers in science or engineering because they are curious about the natural world. Others are motivated by the excitement and beauty of the intellectual world and hope to formulate theories that will lead to new ways of thinking about the world. Careers in science and engineering are essentially hope-filled endeavours that can improve people's lives and result in knowledge that all people can share. As the techniques and products of science and technology have become more central to modern society, a background in science and engineering has become essential to more and more careers.

CAREER IN SCIENCE

Your success will depend on going where your particular interests lead you. Are you exhilarated by the challenge of a new problem or puzzle or need? Does the complexity of the natural world prompt a desire to understand it? If so, science and engineering study-rigorous, though it will provide you with the tools and concepts that you need to achieve your goals. Are you bright enough to become a scientist or engineer? Again, there is no standard against which to measure yourself; no kind of intelligence applies across all the fields of science and engineering. But you can do no more than a trust your deepest feeling. If your enjoyment of mathematics and science is real, you will probably want to understand, use, and explore them at a deeper level.

CAREER IN ENGINEERING

Engineering is a very rewarding and exciting career because engineers help people by designing equipment, tools, transportation systems, and structure and communication devices. Bioengineering is an area of tremendous growth, with many recent advances in medical scanning technologies, artificial organs and implants, and many other devices. Transportation is also changing rapidly with new electric or hybrid vehicles and high-speed systems such as computers and communication devices continue to rapidly increase in capability. The professional career of engineering has great opportunities for travel, for a wide variety in job assignments, and for advancement through management ranks. With the globalization manufacturing, opportunities for travel abound.

An engineer's education in problem solving and in large systems comes in hand management. In high-tech companies the management team is more likely than not comprised of individuals with technical or engineering backgrounds. Engineers carry significant responsibilities and must be competent, since the design of buildings, bridges, airplanes, or automobiles affects the safety of many people. Whereas doctors through rare malpractice may injure one person at a time, engineers can affect the lives of many people all at once.

Engineering technology is defined in many ways. The best definition of engineering technology is the application of engineering principles to common problems. The engineering technology graduate is schooled in both the theory of engineering applications and the application of those theories to the solution of real-world problems encountered in industry. The differences between engineering technology and engineering vary between the disciplines. In the most basic form, engineering technology is less mathematically and scientifically rigorous than engineering.

Many engineering technology applications rely on more basic mathematical and scientific skills for problem solving than does engineering. Engineering Technology graduates are more widely schooled in the practical applications of the mathematical and scientific principles to solve problems than many engineering graduates.

☑ PLAN YOUR CAREER

Everyone needs to straighten out their thoughts concerning the future. Think about yourself. What am I really going to do? Can I really get there? If I don't make it, do I have any other options? Are my subjects appropriate?

Every human being is an individual. The tendency of our physical body different from that of every other person creates a basic of a kind loneliness that is experienced deeply as the adolescent discovers that he is a unique person. The process of career planning stretches through the secondary and senior secondary years at school. Keeping in mind all attributes, preparation to enter a course and career is adequately motivated and effective. Achieve a balanced approach to learning.

When you are choosing a career, you have to consider what you expect from your job -power, money, status, discipline, command or challenge, Interest in the job is absolutely vital for growth in any profession. In choosing a career it is important that you know yourself well, what you want from your profession and also what the world of occupation has to offer.

Get help through career counselling!

RULES TO DECIDE CAREER

- Make a list of work options. Look at these options: see if you have the required support for these realistic options that are open to you at present.
- Expose yourself to wider knowledge by attending career exhibitions and talks, reading and, above all, talking to people in the field of your interests.
- Try to obtain a true description of the work. You need to be alert and sensitive to your inner self and to the opportunities in the future.

Finding the right career is not always that easy. You may have a number of careers in mind, but may not be sure which one is right for you? You might be asking yourself what I am really good at. What skills do I need to do?

Make appropriate and realistic career choices. If you're having trouble deciding what you want to do and where you want to go, whether it is deciding on a course of study, upgrading your existing skills, or finding the right job. Find out about the training or study you need to do for your career choice. Plan a strategy to get work in your chosen field.

BUILD THE FUTURE

We should all be concerned about the future because we will have to spend the rest of our lives there. You *can* get on with your life, and you can put safeguards into place to ensure a better tomorrow. The future is the unexposed portion awaiting images you have yet to experience.

An elderly carpenter was ready to retire. He told his employer-contractor of his plans to leave the house building business and live a more leisurely life with his wife and enjoying his extended family. He would miss the paycheck, but he needed to retire. They could get by.

The contractor was sorry to see his good worker go and asked if he could build just one more house as a personal favour. The carpenter said yes, but in time it was easy to see that his heart was not in his work. He resorted to shoddy workmanship and used inferior materials. It was an unfortunate way to end his career.

When the carpenter finished his work and the builder came to inspect the house, the contractor handed the front-door key to the carpenter. "This is your house," he said, "my gift to you." What a shock! What a shame! If he had only known he was building his own house, he would have done it all so differently. Now he had to live in the house he had built none too well.

So is it with us. We build our lives in a distracted way, reacting rather than acting, willing to put up less than the best. At crucial times we do not give the job our best effort. Then with a shock we look at the situation we have created and find that we are now living in the house we have built. If we had realized that we would have done it differently.

Think of yourself as the carpenter. Think about your house. Each day you hammer a nail, place a board, or erect a wall. Build wisely. It is the only life you will ever build. Even if you live it for only one day more, that day deserves to be lived graciously and with dignity. The plaque on the wall says, "Life is a do-it-yourself project." Your life tomorrow will be the result of your attitudes and the choices you make today.

BRAINWAVE: *Hot heads and cold hearts never solved anything.*

KEEP IN MIND: *Always remember you're unique, just like everyone else.*

THINK ZONE: *Anything I do, I learn about first. I am not in favour of improvisation; I believe in work and in learning.*

6

Time Management

Success and failure depend entirely on how you spend your time. Perhaps two people may succeed at the same thing, but of the two, the person who uses time wisely will be more successful. The difference lies in how you utilize those twenty-four hours. If a person works or studies three times longer than another person in a single day, then he or she is three days ahead of the other person.

Life is too precious to waste; do not take even a moment for granted, for things are built upon the accumulation of moments. Time management is one of the most important aspects of creating successful and productive study habits. In fact, good time management is a crucial element to organizing not only your study time but also your entire life. Take time to deliberate, but when it is time act do not delay.

The French philosopher, Voltaire, asked his followers: "What, of all things, is longest and shortest, slowest and fastest; with it all is possible; without it, nothing?"

TIME!

It is turning every moment of your time into a valuable asset.

- Use your mind and talents fully.
- Be more organized and effective.
- Have more confidence and self worth.
- Be more fulfilled, more satisfied.
- Be more enthusiastic and motivated.

The clock is always ticking, no one can stop it. What will you do with the precious seconds, hours, days and years allotted to you?

I have good news for you. You do have such an account – time account! Every day of your life your account is credited with 1440 precious, priceless minutes. The three rules to regulate your time account:

1. You are the only person who can draw on your time account.
2. You can't carry a balance forward. Whatever time is left in your account, unused at the end of the day, is gone forever. Killing time is success suicide.
3. You can't make an overdraft.

No matter how old or young, how skilled or unpracticed, how knowing or ignorant-we all have a 1440-minute day.

HOW TO SPEND YOUR TIME

Total Time:

- 1 week 168 hours
- 28-day month 672 hours
- 29-day month 696 hours

- 30-day month 720 hours
- 31-day month 744 hours

Include the number of hours and the percentage for each area. The allocations in the four areas added to 100%.

A Family and home activities

- Activities with brother/sister/relative
- Regular home chore
- Common activities
- Family vacations
- Miscellaneous

Time per Week:____
% of Total Time: ____

Time per Month: ____
% of Total Time: ____

B School and Career

- School hours
- School related regular activity at home
- Travel time to go school
- Miscellaneous

Time per Week:____
% of Total Time: ____

Time per Month: ____
% of Total Time: ____

C Social life and environmental contribution

- Social interaction
- Religious practices
- Miscellaneous

Time per Week:____
% of Total Time: ____

Time per Month: ____
% of Total Time: ____

D Health and recreation

- Rest and sleep
- Physical exercises
- Recreation and hobbies
- Playing or walking with friends
- Miscellaneous

Time per Week:____
% of Total Time: ____

Time per Month: ____
% of Total Time: ____

Analyze your results:

Where are you spending time excessively? You can determine your areas of strength and weakness, including your potential seed of failure. It is like having a '**Vitamin deficiency**', with a need to add '**Time supplements**' to bring back your balance. Now you can take remedial action to improve your work efficiency. The most successful people are those who are able to go the extra miles in effort and spend more time doing the most important things that bring the greatest values to life while maintaining balance.

	A	B	C	D
Weekly				
Remedial Action				
Monthly				
Remedial Action				

Do not be a slave to time. Make time work for you, and spend your time wisely. The word 'no' is the single most time management tool you have. Remember it when you have work to do and your friends want to go partying. Just say no until your work is completed. Once you have established good study time management skills, you will have more time to enjoy other activities. Plan your schedule thoroughly. Do not overload yourself. If you do, you are just setting yourself up for failure.

Plan your time wisely and figure in all aspects of your life. Determine what is most important. Set up your educational priority list now.

1. ______________________________
2. ______________________________
3. ______________________________
4. ______________________________

When planning your time, make sure you include the following strategy into your formula. You need to:

- **Play Hard!**
- **Study Hard!**
- **Work Hard!**

THE VALUE OF A SCHEDULE

Before you even begin to think about the process of studying, you must develop a schedule. There's never a wrong time to do the right thing. Be sensitive to place and timing, and plant the right seed at the right time in the right spot. Time, place and circumstances are beyond one's control, in all good or bad luck.

I think that every body who is successful has to be at the right place at the right moment. Don't be afraid to revise your schedule; if your schedule doesn't work, revise it.

TIME BUDGET SHEET

"Time hath a wallet at its back in which it puts alms for oblivion."

—**Shakespeare**

Fill out the time budget sheet which helps you to see where your time is spent.

- Total number of hours available
- Minus hours in class per week
- Minus hours of study time per week
- Minus hours of sleep time/personal exercise / other recreation per week
- Minus hours of family time/ meal time per week

THE TIME BUDGET WORK SHEET

Activity	Mon	Tue	Wed	Thru	Fri	Sat	Sun
Class hours							
Study hours							
Sleep, etc.							
Committed							
Exercise/ Personal							
Family/ Meal time							
Email/ Internet							
Television / Others							

KEY POINTS FOR TIME MANAGEMENT

- Study difficult/boring subjects first
- Plan the day, the week, and the term
- Finish each task before starting another
- Learn to say NO, be assertive with friends
- Avoid interruption; seek the help of experts
- Study with intervals, pace yourself and plan ahead
- Set goals so the emphasis on the tasks important to you

ACTION PLAN

Goal:

____

____

Expected outcome or result:

____

____

Target date for completion:

____

____

Activities	Due Date	Persons Responsible	Resources Needed
1.			
2.			
3.			

If you are happy with what you are achieving, continue with working on your goal. If you find that, it isn't going to fulfill your dream, feel free to restart the process. Yet, know goals are built on steps; you need to take one step at a time, and often the end result isn't fully visible until you have committed yourself fully and given it, your best at all times.

TAKE A QUIET 15-MINUTES

Set aside a certain time each day for doing nothing except quiet thinking and planning. Use this 'quiet epoch' to help you accomplish more every day. Shut the door hang a 'quiet epoch' sign switch off your mobile or forward your phone to voice mail. Do whatever you can to obtain privacy and reach your objective for the day. Your 'quiet epoch' doesn't necessarily need to be 30 consecutive minutes you might want to try two 15-minute sessions, per day. By planning for your future you will achieve your desired results in the most efficient way possible.

BRAINWAVE: *With it, all is possible; without it, nothing!*

KEEP IN MIND: *Take care of the minutes, and the hours will take care of themselves.*

THINK ZONE: *Organizing is what you do before you do something, so that when you do it, it's not all mixed up.*

7

Winning Wave

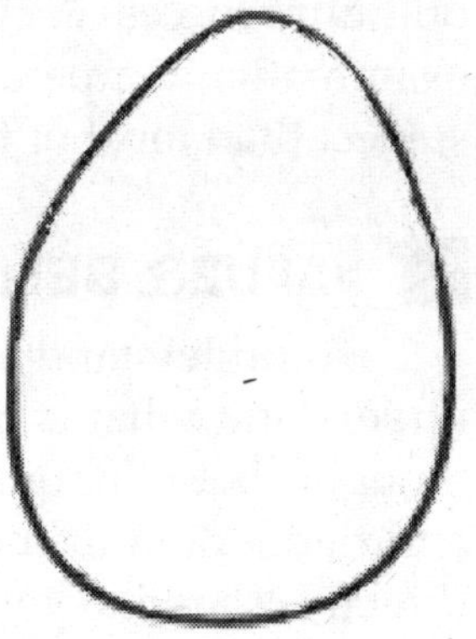

FROM ORDINARY TO EXTRA- ORDINARY

An almighty God does not decide our fate. We decide our own fate by our actions. We achieve everything by our efforts alone. It is not a matter of sitting back and accepting, you have to gain mastery over yourself. Floods, earthquakes, typhoons and all kinds of disasters may hit the world. But what keeps the human race going? It is a powerful force within us, an eternal spring of energy called motivation. It was Lord Buddha's motivation that drove him to give up his princely life in search of nirvana and give the world a new religion. At an individual level, it is positive motivation that elevates us from the ordinary to the extraordinary. If there is only a 1% chance of success in an examination, a true scholar sees that 1% as the spark to light a fire. The spark for creative ideas comes from hard work and positive thinking. "When others start counting the impossibilities, you start counting the possibilities." Count differently: confirm the possibilities, and then quickly work on whatever can turn those possibilities into reality.

The general notion is that the JEE is a difficult examination and the questions are complex and tough, this is not true. It is merely a different exam. To have optimum success & avoid failing, all it requires is a proper examination temperament and different approach to the subject than most of the other exams.

☑ VALUES, BELIEFS, AND DESIRES

To understand what motivates you, you'll need to understand what is important to you. If you have never thought about this question, do it now. Judging the quality and depth of your motivation is important, because it is directly related to your commitment. Often students find that they 'want' a good academic outcome, but they can't seem to make it happen. Sometimes this gap occurs when there is a clash between what they are striving for and what they would rather be doing. It's okay for values, beliefs, and desires to be in conflict, but it is important to recognize when they are and act appropriately. Student needs to both rethink and internalize the relationship of school and dream or he/she needs to change his/her circumstances. But without such a clarification his/her motivation will continue to lag and his/her performance will be less than it should be.

PERSONAL CIRCUMSTANCE

Once you have set goals that match your beliefs, values and desires, you should be in a position to act on them successfully. However, your motivation can be undermined if you fail to consider your circumstances or if your circumstances change, but your goals don't. A goal may match your values and may be realistically set when you begin your academic journey, but may need modification and readjustment as time passes. Unfortunately, when circumstances change, students are often unwilling to make related adjustments in their self-expectations. In these cases, students rarely perform up to their expectations, become frustrated, and lose motivation. However, motivation and performance can be maintained when personal circumstances are taken into account. Students those are willing to redefine their goals to account for their changed circumstances can remain motivated and on the path to success.

SUCCESS FUNDAMENTALS

Visualize yourself achieving each goal. See, hear, smell, touch, and taste the doing of it. Have you ever said to yourself, "I need to study more" or "I wish I had more time to get into a work-out routine?" How about actually accomplishing these things? Why do we fail at achieving our goals more often than we succeed? A big part of it has to do with effective planning. In order to accomplish a goal you have to be deliberate in setting goals and making progress toward goal achievement using your time effectively. This four-step process can help you accomplish this.

1. CREATE A VISION

Where are you headed? Select your destination.

Before you know what you need to accomplish on any given day, you need to have a clear understanding of your overall vision. You must define why are you here? Why are you in school? What do you hope to accomplish in your life? What is really important to you? When creating your personal vision, be ambitious and be specific.

2. SET CONCRETE GOALS

Now set your specific, time bound goals a clear description of desired results of your actions. Once you know what is important to you, you need to set concrete goals. Goals take your personal vision and transform it into achievable tasks. The crucial first step in goal setting is making sure that you have set an achievable goal.

3. DEVELOP A DAILY PLAN

Armed with a personal vision and concrete goals, you are ready to tackle your day-to-day tasks. What you really need to do is learn to manage yourself in the time that you have available to you.

- Spend the last 15 minutes of every night or the first 15 minutes of every morning reviewing what you need to accomplish.
- Review your to-do list daily. Make sure the things on your list are things that are important in accomplishing your goals. Observe that you don't fill up your to-do list with things that help other people get ahead at the expense of accomplishing your own goals.

4. STOP, CHALLENGE, AND CHOOSE

Just because something is difficult doesn't mean that you shouldn't try, it means you should just try harder. Stop, challenge, and choose are the fundamental skills to use to stay on plan. When you don't feel positive about where you are going or you are being pulled backwards, stop and ask yourself: Is this choice; is this feeling, helping me or preventing me in my pursuit toward a goal or action plan? Challenge your irrational thinking. Choose to stay on course.

Persistence is no doubt one of the most valuable attributes in making progress toward a goal. Stop, Challenge, and Choose is a tool of persistence.

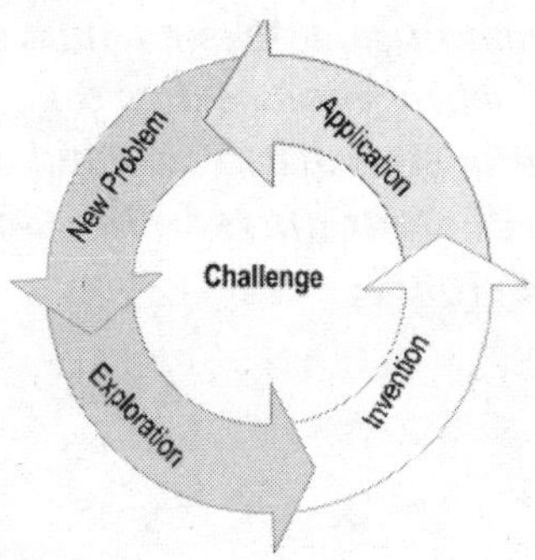

Put this book down. Start working on the most nagging task in your backlog. Don't turn this page until you feel good about the progress you've made.

SAND AND STONE

Two friends were walking through a desert. During some point of the journey they had an argument, and one friend slapped the other one in the face. The one who got slapped was hurt, but without saying anything, wrote in the sand: ***"today my best friend slapped me in the face."***

They kept on walking until they found an oasis, where they decided to take a bath. The one, who had been slapped, got stuck in the mire and started sinking, but the friend saved him. After the friend recovered from the shocked, he wrote on a stone: ***"today my best friend saved my life."***

The friend who had slapped and saved his best friend asked him, "After I hurt you, you wrote in the sand and now, you write on a stone, why?"

The other friend replied: "When someone hurts us, we should write it down in sand where winds of forgiveness can erase it away. But, when someone does something good for us, we must engrave it in stone where no wind can ever erase it."

Learn to write your hurts in the sand, and to carve your blessings in stone.

BRAINWAVE: *To attain knowledge, add things every day. To attain wisdom, remove things everyday.*

KEEP IN MIND: *Concentrate all your thoughts upon the work at hand. The Sun's rays do not burn until brought to a focus.*

THINK ZONE: *The biggest enemy of future success is past success.*

8

Master Move

"I move with the infinite in Nature's Power,
I hold the fire of the soul,
I hold life and healing."

—Rig Veda

KNOW YOUR OWN LIMITS

I wanted a perfect ending. Now I've learnt, the hard way. Some poems don't rhyme. Some stories don't have a clear beginning, middle, or an end. Life is about not knowing, having to change, taking the moment and making the best of it without knowing what's going to happen next. Be truthful with yourself. Know what you expect of yourself. Be realistic about what you can and cannot do. Once you are realistic about your expectations, you are then in a position to take control of them. You should be aware of your needs and expectations and act accordingly. You may feel that there are circumstances that warrant accepting lower performance such as a course is very difficult for you. If you get too far behind or take on more than you can handle, seek help and advice. Sometimes dropping a course that is dealing you problems can be the best solution.

I never like to suggest dropping a course but once you have dropped it, don't have a negative mindset at any stage. Only the dare, dedicated and well determined one can make it. If you want to hit a bird on the wing you must have all your will in focus, you must not be thinking about yourself and, equally, you must not be thinking about your neighbour: you must be living in your eye on that bird; every achievement is a bird on the wing. Once you are on the march of IITJEE then nothing can stop you.

When we have a desire that is not fulfilled, quite commonly we give it up in some way. We stop caring as much, we stop wanting, we stop trusting, when a man stops believing, he will stop caring. When a woman stops believing, she will tend to stop trusting. In both cases, they will give up hope. Hope is vitally important to stay in touch with our ability to feel our desires fully. Trust, caring, and strong desire are the ingredients of power. We need all three.

Yet all this intense feeling doesn't have to rip our lives apart. When we know how to manage our feelings and release negative emotions, intense feeling can be mostly positive.

"Foresight is seeing the way to the goal before taking it or perceiving the uselessness of a certain lead without trying it and hind-sight is observing that a lead is good or bad after trying it."

Think before you hit the ball. What are you going to do? Why are you doing it? Where are you going to hit it? To whom are you going to hit the ball? Let decide yourself, you may fumble and stumble, but that is a process of learning; never get frustrated.

GOAL SETTING

The first and the most important characteristic of the motivated behaviour are energy mobilization. A hungry dog takes the bread even while beaten. When the need is excessive the process of metabolism in the body also increases in the same proportion and the nervous energy increases in the same ratio. A motivated person has a goal, hence he continuously changes his activities with the view of attainment of goal. A man with the goal of earning money tries many ways for it. Sometimes he purchases a lottery ticket while at other times he is busy in some business. In fact the motivated person goes on changing his ways till he arrives at the way successful for the achievement of the aim. In the beginning his behavior is trial and error, but after he knows the successful way he always follows it.

Knowing what you value and desire, along with an assessment of your strengths and weaknesses, makes it possible to establish personal goals. Most people already have a mix of short-term and long-term goals of some type in mind for themselves. It is not unusual for short-term goals to support long-term goals. For example, a student's long-term goal to get in IIT might be supported by a series of short-term goals related to class attendance, study habits, project preparation, academic test performance and commitment to outside activities.

CHARACTERISTICS OF REACHABLE GOALS:

1. **A Reachable Goal Is Realistic.** Set goals that is realistic for your situation, your skills, talents and interests.

2. **A Reachable Goal Is Believable And Possible.** You are the key person here so don't set a goal that you don't believe in. Make sure that you believe you can do it and that it is possible to do in the time you've set aside.
3. **A Reachable Goal Is Measurable.** If your long-term goal is 'to be successful' you will be more likely to reach that goal if you say it in concrete and specific terms. For a weekly goal, move beyond statements like: I want to do better in all my classes. Instead, promise your self that you will read two chapters of Physics by Saturday.
4. **A Reachable Goal Is Flexible.** Sometimes our plans change; sometimes we get sick. Be prepared to reassess and revise your goal if necessary. If you are too sick to study, you may have to revise your goal of reading two chapters of Physics by extending the time to Monday.
5. **A Reachable Goal Is Controllable.** Make sure you are in charge of your goal. If friends suggest that the best way to pass a class is to study old tests but you know your learning style demands chapter outlines to get the material down, stick with what works for you and in your control.

MAKE TIME TO THINK LIKE GENIUS

A young and successful executive was driving down a neighbourhood street, going a bit too fast in his new Jaguar. He was watching out for kids darting out from between parked cars

and slowed down when he thought he saw something. As his car passed, no children appeared. Instead, a brick smashed into the Jag's side door! He slammed on the brakes and drove the Jag back to the spot where the brick had been thrown. The angry driver then jumped out of the car, grabbed the nearest kid and pushed him up against a parked car, shouting, "What was that all about and who are you? Just what the heck are you doing? That's a new car and that brick you threw is going to cost a lot of money. Why did you do it?"

The young boy was apologetic. "Please sir... please, I'm sorry... I didn't know what else to do," he pleaded.

"I threw the brick because no one else would stop..." With tears dripping down his face and off his chin, the youth pointed to a spot just around a parked car. "It's my brother," he said.

"He rolled off the curb and fell out of his wheelchair and I can't lift him up."

Now sobbing, the boy asked the stunned executive, "Would you please help me get him back into his wheelchair? He's hurt and he's too heavy for me."

Moved beyond words, the driver tried to swallow the rapidly swelling lump in his throat. He hurriedly lifted the handicapped boy back into the wheelchair, then took out his fancy handkerchief and dabbed at the fresh scrapes and cuts. A quick look told him everything was going to be okay.

"Thank you and May God bless you," the grateful child told the stranger. Too shaken up for words, the man simply watched the little boy push his wheelchair-bound brother down the sidewalk toward their home. It was a long, slow walk back to the Jaguar. The damage was very noticeable, but the driver never bothered to repair the dented side door. He kept the dent there to remind him of this message: Don't go through life so fast that someone has to throw a brick at you to get your attention!

God whispers in our souls and speaks to our hearts. Sometimes when we don't have time to listen, He has to throw a brick at us. It's our choice: Listen to the whisper ... or wait for the brick!

BRAINWAVE: *Accept good advice gracefully as long as it doesn't interfere with what you intend to do.*

KEEP IN MIND: *As it turns out, now is the moment you've been waiting for.*

THINK ZONE: *When you're over the hill that's when you pick up speed.*

9
Right Time

NOTHING IS IMPOSSIBLE

It is only your lack of tenacity that makes it seem impossible.

Whether they are athletes, artists, or business leaders, great performers appear to have several outstanding characteristics in common: commitment, discipline, passion, vision, perseverance, confidence, creativity, and willpower. Possibilities are hiding in every area, and it is up to you to discover them. Life opens its doors to those who are positive, those that have confidence and faith, and those who challenge life with energy. Robert Schuller said, "everything we have today was at one time considered impossible." Entire thing was made possible because people had faith and confidence in themselves, and such people continue to mould history. Nothing could be a greater waste of time and energy than someone who has the capabilities to become a great musician neglecting those talents and sitting around whining that he or she does not have the ability to become a great painter. I believe that people are born with tremendous capabilities and that they were created to use those capabilities. Visualize whatever it is you want to do, and you can do it, if you put your mind to it. I believe everyone has unlimited capabilities, but they are often not tapped except in extraordinary situations.

WHEN TO START:

Confucius said, ***'the longest journey begins with a single step.'*** If you want to get in IIT just after class XII then you should start planning at the right time even after class VIII. And there is no harm because you must keep in mind the story of the hare and the tortoise as slow and steady win the race. You are on the march nothing can stop you.

First buy the NCERT Science and Mathematics books. Try to complete them during summer break before the school restarts. If you take a look at the syllabus of IITJEE you will find that a number of lessons are taught at introductory level in class IX and class X. These topics at advanced level are then taught in class XI and class XII: Physics, Chemistry and Mathematics. Buy some relevant Physics, Chemistry and Mathematics books and also Science dictionary. Spend one and half-hours specifically for IITJEE studies, if you want to be a part of the world top technocrats.

Never compromise on quality education. Take guidance only from experienced educationists. Don't depend on commercial coaching associations or the frustrated youth who provide coaching only to make money. Instead engage in self study. Today a lot of instructors but few are real teachers; as teachers have lost their sense of social mission. Read the interviews with successful candidates.

When you are in class X give more emphasis on Mathematics because Mathematics provides a platform for building technology and expanding the application area of engineering. Try to understand the definitions, laws, derivations, units and dimensions of physical quantities in science. This is true for IIT-JEE as well, where one has to put his/her maximum efforts, to have a cutting edge over other competitors, in order to achieve a top rank in the merit list.

Mathematics is used as a tool to evaluate the potential of future technocrats. The mathematics section of IIT-JEE is multi-dimensional and multi-purpose. Multi-dimensional refers to identifying hidden facts and implementing the mathematical concept to formulate and decide the suitable presentation form of the solution, based on the options given for a particular problem. Multipurpose refers to the evaluation of candidate's analytical ability and thoroughness on the concepts of allied sections. An exhaustive section the mathematics section requires wide application of mathematical concepts of class X level. One will be required to apply elementary algebra in trigonometry, calculus, co-ordinate geometry and of course higher algebra.

PREPARATION STRATEGY

The study of mathematics can be divided into three areas:

1. Concepts or hypothesis,
2. Physical/geometrical significance or meaning
3. And the implication of concepts/ hypothesis.

The strategy should be multi-stage. The first stage should cover terminology, concepts, hypothesis, and relations. The physical/ geometrical significance/ meaning should be covered in the second stage. The wide coverage of implications of concepts in the last stage raises the level of excellence to crack the IIT-JEE problems. But one should have enough practise on simpler problems before venturing into the last stage.

DEVELOPMENTAL LEVELS OF LEARNING FOR IIT-JEE:

Do not dilute preparation of any topic because of any factor etc. Unlike school/board exams you cannot score in IIT-JEE without reaching a certain level of proficiency. Mere understanding of a concept is not adequate. You have to learn to apply these concepts in solving tricky problems. Problems in IIT-JEE are not direct application of a single concept. Many IIT-JEE problems involve more than one basic concept.

- **Step I: Concrete Experience:** Learn basic concepts and their applications.
- **Step II: Observation and Reflection:** Learn application of numerous concepts of particular Sub-disciplines of a subject in a single problem.
- **Step III: Forming Abstract Concepts:** Learn application of several concepts of a subject in a single problem.

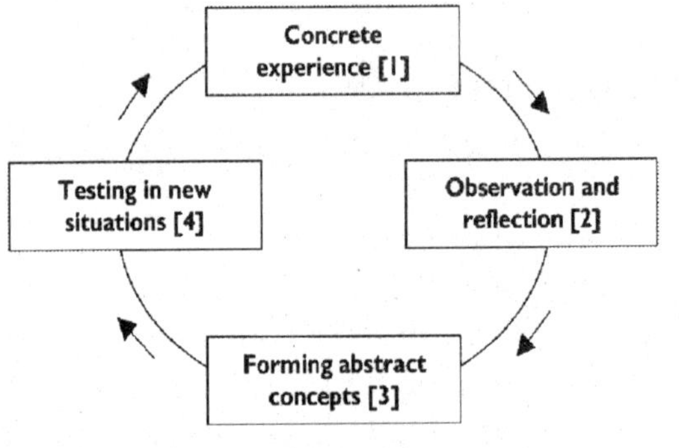

- **Step IV: Testing in New Situation:** Learn application of numerous concepts of a subject in a single problem where information from another subject matter is also to be used.

WORK AREA

The work area needs to be a well-planned and thought-out area. Design and arrange it to be as comfortable as possible. When setting up the work area, remember comfort is very important since many hours will be spent studying there. The work area should contain a desk with a spacious worktop; the top should allow you to spread out books, notebooks, and other needed materials. You will need a lamp on or near the desk; also make sure you select a comfortable chair. This will help lessen some eyestrain and eliminate fatigue. The work area needs to be stocked with the following supplies: sharpened pencils, ball point pens, felt tip pens, highlighters, papers, stapler, paper clips, pencil sharpener, a scientific calculator, a log table, a dictionary, thesaurus, and a set of encyclopedias if possible.

HOW TO GET STARTED:

Believe you can succeed. Be willing to pay the price. The price is always what you don't want to pay. Failure begins in an excuse, a short cut. People who want to become the best try their very best. If you try your best, you may not always come out on top, but you will come close to it. What you are doing is important, but not as important as how you go about it; your attitude should be one of becoming the best in whatever you are doing. I believe that everyone who is at number one in his field got there because he aimed high and tried his best.

Many years ago a Hungarian soccer star interviewed

after his team captured first place in a European competition. Out of the times he had, he would play soccer; when he was not kicking a soccer ball, he was talking about soccer; and when he was not talking about soccer, he was thinking about it.

Countless times students have asked me what is the best way to study. I like to think of studying to the point of mastery of the material as a process very much like climbing a ladder. You will never get to the top unless you can hold on to each rung of the ladder. Typical study methods force you to start at the bottom rung each time. But how can you reach the top (mastery) in just one study session? The answer is you can't. So, you must find a way to hold on to the rung you had reached during your last effort. While the recommendations that I am about to make to you are no guarantee of success, I believe they will optimize your chances of success.

☑ TO BE SUCCESSFUL IN SCHOOL

Research shows that the average student will study for a test. The average person will study four hours for a daily quiz, four hours for a weekly quiz, four hours for a major test, four hours for a midterm, and four hours for a comprehensive final. The outcome of these four hours of study will vary from and for a daily quiz to the comprehensive final. This means that in high school grades are strongly determined by intelligence since everyone studies the same amount of time. The brain does not process and store information the way that students prefer studying. Occasionally, some succeed by studying at the last minute, but they are exceptions to the rule.

Research suggests that the slowest 10 percent of the students may need 5 to 6 times as much time to learn the same material as the fastest 10 percent. Each person is highly likely to have strengths and weaknesses. Overcoming your weakness increases your strength. In other words, you can succeed if you pay the price necessary for success. You have the right to fail as long as you have tried your best. If a person never tastes failure, how can he or she expect to taste success?

- Success isn't easy. Success in school requires studying-lots of it. Though you may find studying a chore, the reality is that it's great satisfaction in mastering a subject area.
- Tests are one method of measuring what you have learned in a course. Doing well on tests and earning good grades begin with good study habits.

WORK SHEET FOR CLASS IX / X STUDENTS:

Based on extensive observation of students performance in academic tests and IITJEE

Examination	Total Hours	Daily Hours	For Academic	For IITJEE	Months
After VIII/IX in Summer Break	150	3	120	30	May & June
Quarterly	120	2.5	100	20	July & August
Half yearly	210	2.5	170	40	Sept., Oct. & Nov.
Yearly	325	3	300 School/ Board	25	Dec., Jan., Feb. & March

BRAINWAVE: *The most important thing about getting somewhere is starting right where we are.*

KEEP IN MIND: *Capabilities get you started. Performance completes the task.*

THINK ZONE: *You must be the change you wish to see in the world.*

10

Inner Voice

☑ HOW'S YOUR PERSONAL RATING?

If you want to improve yourself, do not detest a well-wisher pointing your fault. Do not afraid to admit you are imperfect. Your dissatisfaction can be a healthy sign. Don't say you are poor and less intelligent: therefore you cannot make a contribution to the world. Sydney Smith said long ago, "A Great deal of talent is lost in the world for the want of a little courage." You can build a more efficient world by building a more efficient YOU! Michael Faraday, the son of a blacksmith, was in early age apprenticed to a bookbinder and worked at that trade until he reached his twenty-second year. He came to occupy the first rank as a scientist, excelling even his master Sir Humphry Davy. Shakespeare sprang from humble rank. His father was a butcher and a grazer, and Shakespeare himself is supposed to have been in early life a wool comber. That includes you too, very often we notice how quickly and smartly we react to emergencies. The hidden powers that lie dormant in us shoot out to work wonders.

DON'T BE AFRAID TO FAIL

130 years ago, an idea changed your world. It was Thomas A. Edison's motivation that snuffed out ten thousand failures and, finally, switched on the incandescent electric light to beam the great electrical age into our lives and homes. You've failed many times, although you may not remember. You fell down the first time you tried to walk. Did you hit the ball the first time you swung a bat? Neither get satisfied with present accomplishments, and nor stop striving for greater heights, because I realize that trying your best in everything that you do is the only way to avoid regrets.

- The world's top batsman Sachin failed to score number of times.
- The ever time superstar Amitab Bachhan rolled in number of movies those flopped.
- English novelist John Creasey got 753 rejection slips before he published 564 books.
- The maximum tenure Indian PM Indira Gandhi lost even her assembly seat in 1977.
- In 1832- Abraham Lincoln lost his Job.
  In 1832- He failed in his business.
  In 1833- He was elected to legislature.
  In 1834- His sweetheart died.
  In 1836- He was defeated for Speaker.
  In 1838- He was defeated for nomination for Congress.
  In 1843- He was elected to Congress.
  In 1848- He was rejected for land officer.

In 1849- He was defeated when he contested for a Senate.
In 1854- He was defeated for nomination for Vice President.

In 1860, Abraham Lincoln was elected the 16th president of the United States of America! So, Commit to your goals—and to yourself!

Persistence and perseverance to achieve a goal are never a waste of time. "You are the only one that can stop you from reaching your goals." Those who say: can't and impossible will do well to learn the philosophy from the poem.

If you think you are beaten, you are.
If you think that you dare not – you don't.
If you'd like to win but think you can't.
It's almost a cinch you won't.
If you think you'll lose- you've lost.

Don't wait for a crisis to discover your hidden abilities, develop it in every day life to enrich the lives of others as well as your own.

If a man is progressive, eager and receptive and ever planning to improve, he will lead others. To remain at the top, you have to work much harder than those behind you. All they need to do is imitate you to catch up.

☑ DON'T QUIT

Don't quit when the tide is lowest, for it's just about to turn,
Don't quit over doubts and questions, for there's something you may learn,
Don't quit when the night is darkest, for it's just a while until dawn.

Don't quit when you've run the farthest, for the race
is almost won.
Don't quit when the hill is steepest, for your goal is
almost nigh,
Don't quit, for you're not a failure, Until you fail to
try.

Persist. Fight. Survive. Don't even think about quitting.

" I tell you, there comes one moment, once and God help those who pass that moment by!"

—Cyrano de Bergerac

STATE OF THE COMMON ASPIRANT

Study for IITJEE is different; in almost all IITJEE courses if you have a poor subjective knowledge and do not really like to read, you are in serious trouble. Your study habits formed in high school may vector you toward failure because you have never experienced what it takes to perform at the IITJEE level. That is why the freshman year is the hardest year you will ever experience in IITJEE is. It takes about one year to learn how to learn at the IITJEE level. Most of the students are highly intelligent and some are highly motivated. Many students have a deep-rooted feeling that they do not stand to succeed in IIT-JEE if they have not been doing extremely well in studies so far. IIT-JEE requires an analytical approach and it is quite different from normal studies.

Students with high **IQ** level can extract the information from the teacher even in a large group, plethora of books and study material available. Other students get confused due to flood of information and study material. One needs to have a definite plan with well-defined helps and sources of information to produce optimum results. Students normally neglect Chemistry, which is most scoring. Preparing Physics for the JEE needs more attention besides acquiring highly polished analytical skills; don't forget the queen mother of all sciences that is Mathematics.

Only think! If you are dedicated—and ready to do hard work with just one dream 'Success at IIT-JEE'. With this book you are sure to gain that confidence, those skills which go into the making of a JEE ranker. Cooperation of parents and dedicated hard work of students are very essential to achieve the goal. **On the basis of our strategic and comprehensive course coverage, years of teaching experience and the results I have produced, I confidently expect an average student who sincerely follows given advises to crack IIT-JEE with a good rank.**

I have planned your academics in such a way that course will be finished much in advance of actual JEE. That will leave enough time for self-revision, polishing of examination temperament and removal of last moment doubts. **You will find a very powerful system that can help you unfold your full potential, systematically.**

BIG ROCKS

One day an expert in time management was speaking to a group of business students and, to drive home a point, used an illustration those students will never forget. As he stood in front

of the group of high-powered overachievers he said, "Okay, time for a quiz". Then he pulled out a gallon, a wide mouthed jar and set it on the table in front of him. Then he produced about a dozen fist-sized rocks and carefully placed them, one at a time, into the jar. When the jar was filled to the top and no more rocks would fit inside, he asked, "Is this jar full?" Everyone in the class said, "Yes." Then he said, "Really?" He reached under the table and pulled out a bucket of gravel. Then he dumped some gravel in and shook the jar causing pieces of gravel to work themselves down into the space between the big rocks. Then he asked the group once more, "Is the jar full?" By this time the class was on to him. "Probably not," one of them answered. "Good!" he replied.

He reached under the table and brought out a bucket of sand. He started dumping the sand in the jar and it went into all of the spaces left between the rocks and the gravel. Once more he asked the question, "Is this jar full?" "No!" the class shouted. Once again he said, "Good." Then he grabbed a pitcher of water and began to pour it in until the jar was filled to the edge. Then he looked at the class and asked, "What is the point of this illustration?" One eager beaver raised his hand and said, "The point is, no matter how full your schedule is, if you try really hard you can always fit some more things in it".

"No," the speaker replied, "That's not the point. The truth this illustration teaches us is: If you don't put the big rocks in first, you'll never get them in at all." What are the 'big rocks' in your life? Your loved ones; Your education; Your dreams; A worthy cause; teaching or mentoring others; Doing things that you love; Time for yourself; Your health; Your significant other. Remember to put these BIG ROCKS in first or you'll never get them in at all. So, tonight, or in the morning, when you are reflecting on this short story, ask yourself this question: What are the 'big rocks' in my life? Then, put those in your jar first.

WORK SHEET FOR CLASS XI / XII STUDENTS

Based on extensive observation of students performance in academic tests and IITJEE

Examination	Total Hours	Daily Hours	For Academic	For IITJEE	Months
After X/XI in	200	4	150	50	May & June
Quarterly	175	3.5	110	65	July & August
Half yearly	275	4	125	150	Sept., Oct. & Nov.
Yearly	370	4	275 School/ Board Exams	95	Dec., Jan., Feb. & March
JEE	100	9		300	April

WORK SHEET FOR THE DROPPERS:

Based on extensive observation of students performance in IITJEE

Class	Total Hours	Monthly Hours	Daily Hours	Months
After XII, in Summer Break	270	135	5	June & July
I Stage	600	150	6	August, Sept., Oct. & Nov.
II Stage	475	175	7	Dec., Jan. & Feb
III Stage	300	195	9	March, April

BRAINWAVE: *My parents told me, "Finish your dinner. People in India are starving. "I tell my children," Finish your homework. People in country are suffering for lack of jobs."*

KEEP IN MIND: *A winner never quits, and a quitter never wins, reasons you can change. Excuses change you.*

THINK ZONE: *If we were born knowing everything, what would we do with all this time on this earth?*

11

Fast Memorize

Your mind is a canvas – you get to experiment and play. Close your eyes and paint an imaged red apple in the middle of a white canvas in your mind: You mentally paint an image. We do this all the time when we remember what something looks like. Visual thinking means seeing, within your mind's eye, clear pictures. Like a zoom lens, your mind can focus close up or take in a wide-angle view.

We talk all the time in our heads. The question is; are we talking positively to ourselves and to the imagined world around us? This is the process of forming pictures of the emotions and sensations in your mind.

Through my teaching, supervising and administrative experience at Institute and School, I have developed, with the help of my colleagues, flexible study skills. We realize that memory is a system of domains - working with different types of information in different ways - we have made a tremendous step forward in understanding memory and in being able to use it more effectively. Memory is thought of as a thing, as a filing system, as a library, as a computer database. But memory is far more complex than that. Some people are blessed with exceptionally good memories, and they can do whatever they do with seemingly little effort. But those people are few and far between. The rest of us have to work at it. Combine good mnemonics techniques with self-hypnosis and you can remember anything.

Believe Me!

☑ READ TO EXTRACT THE IMPORTANT DETAILS AND MAIN IDEA

A primary means by which you acquire information is through reading. In college you're expected to do much more reading than in high school. Don't assume just because you've 'read' the assignments that is the end of it. You must learn to read with a purpose to extract details to locate main ideas.

- You must know before you begin reading what your purpose is, and read accordingly
- You must learn what the author's central idea is, and understand it in your own way
- You must Identify main ideas in multi-paragraph selections

☑ READING, UNDERLINING, AND TAKING NOTES:

As you read the material, you must underline the important points and take notes. Use only the left half of the page. Transfer to the right side of the paper comments your teacher made about the material during lecture. You must always be ahead of your teacher in your reading. The process of reading and deciding; the material that is important enough should be underlined as it increases memory of that material. It is the decision and thinking that creates the memory.

Take over your note making abilities. Do you consider them to be good, weak, or just down right poor? To help you think about them and get a better idea and picture of them, take a few minutes and complete the following exercise.

The strongest points of my note taking are:

____

____

____

____

The weakest points of my note taking are:

____

____

____

____

Knowing this information can help strengthen and improve your note taking skills.

THE AAURR METHOD

The AAURR method has been a proven way to sharpen study skills. **AAURR stands for Analyze, Ask, Understand, Recite, than Review.**

ANALYZE - get the best overall picture of what you're going to study **before** you study its any detail. It's like looking at a road map before going on a trip. If you don't know the territory, studying a map is the best way to begin. Before you start your learning task, read over the major headings and summaries of the chapters in the textbook.

ASK - ask questions for learning. The important things to learn are usually answers to questions. Questions should lead to emphasis on the, why, how, when, who and where of study content. Ask yourself questions as you read or study. As you answer them, you will help to make sense of the material and remember it more easily because the process will make an impression on you.

UNDERSTAND - Reading is NOT running your eyes over a textbook but to understand. When you read, read actively. Read to answer questions you have asked yourself or questions the author has asked. Always be alert to **bold** or *italicized* print. When you read, be sure to read everything, including tables, graphs and illustrations. Often times tables, graphs and illustrations can convey an idea more powerfully than text.

RECITE - When you recite, you stop reading periodically to recall what you have read. Try to recall main headings, important ideas of concepts presented in bold or italicized type, and what graphs charts or illustrations indicate. Try to develop an overall concept of what you have read in your own words and thoughts. **Try to connect things you have just read to things you already know**.

REVIEW - A review is a survey of what you have covered. It is a review of what you are supposed to accomplish, not what you are going to do. Rereading is an important part of the review process. Reread with the idea that you are measuring what you have gained from the process. **The best time to review is when you have just finished studying something.**

TIPS FOR IMPROVING YOUR MEMORY

- Avoid pressuring yourself. Forgetting important

things is frustrating, but worrying about it can make it worse.

- Depression can affect memory, as well as the ability to think. If you suspect, consult your doctor.
- Eat right and exercise. Establish a routine.
- Do one activity at a time.
- Take notes. Post them in appropriate places to trigger your memory. Make a daily list of things to do.
- Be aware of stress and fatigue.

LEARNING AND RECALLING INSTANTLY AND QUICKLY

Our thoughts and memories will stay in our minds forever, all of them, good and bad. The mistakes, embarrassing incidents, false / wrong information, fears, phobias, childhood, laughter, love and happy times, they are all there forever, although we may at times have difficulty recalling them at will. Repeating something, then recalling it the next day, starts to make a 'groove' in the brains pathways. Each time that we recall something it deepens the 'groove', and if this happens many times it will seem permanently 'etched' into our brain.

Elderly people often say I can remember things from many years ago, even way back to childhood, far better than what happened last week. But this does not mean their memory is faulty. For so long as it is healthy it is as good as it ever was. It is just that older people feel a lot of pleasure in thinking back over their lives and 'reliving' events and experiences. Each time they do so it keeps those memories 'grooves' fresher than the mundane happenings of the previous week's memories. It is a myth that memory and thinking powers decline with age.

Keeping body and mind healthy just needs regular gentle exercise that make the heart beat a little faster and keeps the blood reaching all parts of the brain.

I started out with the world's worst ability to concentrate or remember anything. That all changed dramatically, when I discovered a few well-kept secrets about how to make concentration and memory better. One of the things I remember most about my childhood is how I could not remember anything. At least I think that was how it was. I really don't remember. Seriously, not many people could claim to have a worse ability to remember than I had when I was a kid. Dates, facts, anything that was important (whether it was academic or not) were almost impossible for me to remember. By the time I was a young adult I was less scatter-brained but I still couldn't remember things very well. My hypnosis skills were still very crude, but I began to use suggestion in combination with the mnemonic techniques. They often change dramatically once they learn how. Really!

BRAINWAVE: *Learning should be done for the sake of learning. Do not substitute memorization for learning.*

KEEP IN MIND: *A winner never quits, and a quitter never wins, reasons you can change. Excuses change you.*

THINK ZONE: *The mark of a good book is it changes every time you read it.*

12
Probe Physics

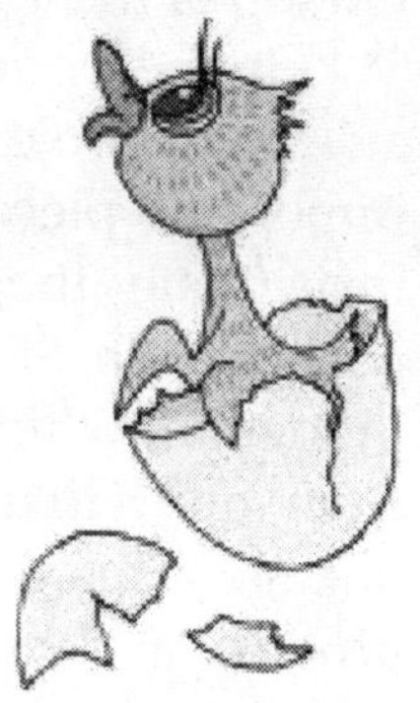

PHYSICS

The science concerned with fundamental relationship between matter and energy. Classical physics developed in 19th century, deals with electricity, magnetism, heat, optics, mechanics, etc. Quantum physics of 20th century, which assumes that energy exists in discrete bundles, explains atomic and nuclear phenomenon.

COMMENTARY ON PHYSICS

PHYSICS is the only subject which changes the WORLD from agony to asylum, shelter and place to enjoy the life in all dimensions. In today's world we rely increasingly on electricity, for communications as well as to operate the equipment we use. Electric currents allow us to transfer energy over great distances and deliver the energy to where it is needed; using the devices, such as generators, transformers and motors and operated by electromagnetic interactions. Many items of equipment that we rely on every day are controlled by microelectronic devices- just think of telephones, radio and television, traffic lights, domestic appliances such as washing machines and freezers, control systems in all forms of transport systems, railway signaling and aircraft control. On top of this there is all the computer equipment in use.

In the world of science, artificial magnetic fields play an essential role. The particle accelerator is one of the most important pieces of equipment used by physicists to investigate the fundamental structure of sub-atomic particles. In 1831 Faraday discovered electromagnetic induction, which enabled him to transfer electric power from one circuit to another by varying the magnetic linkage. This discovery made it possible for Faraday to produce and distribute electrical energy. The fire, police and ambulance services all need to respond swiftly to calls, and this often means driving as fast as possible through heavy traffic to the scene of an emergency. Technology used in high speed trains reduces fuel costs due to reduced friction: friction with the air is kept low, while friction with track is set at a sufficiently high level for safety. A modern vehicle with low drag traveling at high speed experiences the same kind of force that allows aircraft to fly – aerodynamic lift.

Success in long jumping comes from a combination of the right body build, hard training and natural skill. In order to try to reach maximum; projection angle should be 45^0. The most powerful natural mechanical waves, and so potentially the most devastating, are those caused by earthquakes. Preventing a high-rise building from toppling is difficult enough, but stopping the collapse of flyovers has proved particularly tricky by the physicist.

Life is based on chemical reactions that can occur only within a limited range of temperature—a range experienced by most places on Earth. However, these temperatures often don't suit humans: think of all the energy we use to heat (or cool) our homes and workplace to a level that we find comfortable. Thermal effects are important in devices that do work, such as steam turbines, petrol engines and diesel engines. The relation between heating and working is brought together in thermodynamics.

Optical lenses, such as the lenses in a camera, viewfinder, photocopier, a telescope or a microscope, allow us to see the images of a wide range of objects. Micro lenses are also used in producing the image on the liquid crystal display (LCD) screen of a portable laptop computer. With its communications revolution, the twentieth century may be remembered as the age of communications. Even school girls and boys are using mobile phones with video; when music groups perform on stage, they no longer have to put with a clutter of wires and speakers because of the progress made in electronic engineering; even musicians need not suffer from hearing damage because they can control their own sound level.

☑ GETTING AN OVERVIEW

Among students, physics as a subject is difficult but once interest is created in it, it becomes the favourite one. You, again like many students, may seem overwhelmed by new terms and equations. You may not have had extensive experience with problem solving and may get lost when trying to apply information from your textbook and classes to an actual physics problem. I hope this book will help! It's designed to help you stay out of the difficulties that come when you think small and get too involved in memorizing formulas or other specific details without understanding the principles fundamentals. It's important to recognize that physics is a problem-solving discipline. You should focus on this fact, that in the physics subject, you are expected to solve problems

TIPS TO KEEP UP WITH COURSE

These tips and suggestions will take more time and effort than does a casual reading of the text, but they will pay off in a savings of time when you do the problems, in a better understanding of physics, and in increasing confidence on exams.

Once you fall behind it is very difficult to catch up. If you ignore this advice and do fall behind, and if you cannot manage the time to do a thorough job of catching up, then skim the passed-over course material for its most important points and move on to a thorough study of the current course material.

- Do the reading before attending the lectures. This way you won't need to take notes on everything the lecturer says, because you will already understand some of the material and you will know that some of it is treated well in your textbook.
- Make groups in the course and use them for discussion, problem suggestions, and companionship. Throw ideas into the group's 'pot' as well as drawing ideas from it. Do not use your study group as a crutch.
- Do not memorize. In almost all cases, the temptation to memorize indicates a simple lack of understanding. In the words "The equation

$F = ma$ is easy to memorize, hard to use, and even more difficult to understand."

READING YOUR PHYSICS TEXTBOOK

Reading the text and solving homework problems is a cycle: Questions lead to answers that lead back to more questions. An entire chapter will often be devoted to the consequences of a single basic principle. You should look for these basic principles.

- Read actively with questions in mind. A passive approach to reading physics wastes your time. Read with a pencil and paper beside the book to jot down questions and notes.
- Stop periodically to go over the important points and recall the material that you have read. During your reading you will notice sections, equations, or ideas that apply directly to assigned problems. Active reading also involves exploring the possibilities of what is being read.

EFFECTIVE PARTICIPATION IN A PHYSICS CLASS

It's important that you be well prepared for class in order to use its potential fully for integrating the course material.

- Read the introduction and the summary of the relevant chapter and look at the section headings and subheadings. Try to formulate questions in your mind about the topics to be covered.
- Examine the drawings and pictures. Try to determine what principles they illustrate.
- Make notes of new words, new units of measure, statements of general laws, and other new concepts.

DURING CLASS:

Come to the class on time and stay till the very end. Often teachers give helpful hints in the first and last minutes of the lecture. Unfortunately, these times are when a lot of people are not listening. Take good notes. It's helpful to draw up a set of abbreviations and use them consistently in taking notes. Leave ample margins for later comments.

- When you copy drawings, completeness is worth more than careful artwork. You should not only copy what are on the board but also record important points that the teacher makes orally about the diagram.
- If you get behind in your note taking, leave a space in your notes and go on. You can fill in your notes later with the help of a classmate or your textbook.
- Ask questions. Don't be embarrassed to ask your teacher questions.

AFTER CLASS:

- Immediately after class, or as soon as possible, review and edit your notes. You need not rewrite them. Rather, you should look for important ideas and relationships among major topics. Summarize these in the margin or on the opposite side if you've taken notes only on one side, and at this time you may want to add an outline to your notes, integrate notes from your textbook.
- As you review your notes, certain questions may come to your mind, then either ask the teacher or try with your friends.

MODE TO APPROACH A PHYSICS PROBLEM:

You may now be like many students a novice problem solver. Effective, expert problem solving involves answering following questions:

- What's the problem about?
- What am I asked to find?
- What information am I to use? What principles apply?
- What do I know about similar situations?
- How can I apply the information to solve the problem?

The goal of this section is to help you become an expert problem solver:

1. Establish which general principle relates the given parameters to the quantity that you are seeking. Usually your picture will suggest the correct techniques and formulas. At times it may be necessary to obtain further information from your textbook or notes before the proper formulas can be chosen.
2. Draw a second picture that identifies the coordinate system and origin that will be used in relating the data to the equations. In some situations this second picture may be a graph, free body diagram, or vector diagram rather than a picture of a physical situation.
3. Do the calculation using the given values from the start, so that the algebra gives numerical values at each intermediate step on the way to the final solution.
4. Gain experience in problem solving by substituting the numbers when you start physics, but gradually adopt the formal approach as you become more confident.
5. Criticize your solution: Ask yourself, "Does it make sense?" Compare your solution to any available examples. Often you can check yourself by doing an approximate calculation. Many times

a calculation error will result in an answer that is obviously wrong, use calculator to check, and be sure to check the units also.

6. In an examination, you may have to do problems under a strict time limitation. Therefore, practise doing them faster, in order to build up your speed and your confidence.

Don't search through your book for 'the right equation'. You will not be able to solve your problem by finding an appropriate equation and then plugging numbers into it.

☑ EFFECTIVE TEST PREPARATION

If you have followed an active approach to study similar to the one suggested in this book, your preparation for exams will not be overly difficult. Always remember: Physics, and therefore physics exams, involve problem solving; so give stress on problem solving. Here are some principles:

1. In the week prior to the exam, Review your notes and recheck the course outline. Your goal at this point is to make sure you know what has been emphasized. Reread your solutions to the homework problems. Remember that these solutions, if complete, will note underlying principles or laws. Review the assigned chapters.
2. If samples of previous exams are available, look them over, also, but do not assume that only previous types of problems will be included. It definitely helps to work with others at this stage.
3. Review actively; including self-tests in which you create your own problems, which involve a combination of principles. You need to be sure that you can work problems without referring to

your notes or to the textbook.

4. Remember that exams will include a variety of different problems. You want to look back on an exam and say, "I know how to do friction problems so well, that even though they were asked in a weird way, I could recognize them and solve them."

BRAINWAVE: *We Could Live At The Present Day Without A Plato, But A Double Number Of Newtons Is Required To Discover The Secrets Of Nature, And To Bring Life Into Harmony With The Laws Of Nature.*

KEEP IN MIND: *Physics is the subject, which changes the world.*

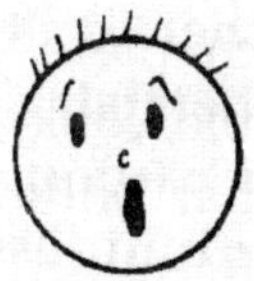

THINK ZONE: *We can easily forgive a child who is afraid of the dark. The real tragedy of life is when an adult is afraid of the light.*

13

Create Chemistry

CHEMISTRY

The science concerned with composition of substances and their reaction with one another. It is divided into organic, inorganic and physical chemistry. Organic chemistry deals with compounds of carbon, excluding metal carbonates and oxides and sulphides of carbon. Inorganic chemistry deals with elements and their compounds, excluding organic carbon compounds. Physical chemistry is application of physical measurements and laws to chemical measurement.

WHAT ROLE DOES CHEMISTRY PLAY IN OUR LIFE

Chemistry is about understanding chemicals; everything we see, touch, smell or taste is made up of chemicals. Many of us live longer and in more comfort than a century ago because of the chemicals we manufacture, such as fertilizers which enable us to grow more food, drugs which combat disease, polymers which clothe us and fuels which keep us warm and transport us. All our body parts are composed of chemicals, from the DNA of cell nuclei to the protein enzymes which catalyze almost all of the reactions which support our very existence.

Chemists have changed our world and transformed almost every aspect of our daily lives by understanding the properties of chemicals and in so doing they are making millions of new ones. Computers, telephones and televisions and much more devices are at the centre of a communications and information revolution; none of these would have existed without the materials those have been developed and manufactured by chemists. Chemists are beginning to discover molecules that can be made to act like the memory of a computer which stores binary information by switching between two states: ON or OFF.

Each part needs different type elements with different properties; it is the job of chemists to get the balance of composition and treatment that suits a specific need. Many thousands of compounds are screened for any biological activity before a promising compound is found. Airbags are a familiar addition to car safety these days, but crashes happen very fast, so how does the airbag inflate in time to protect the drives from injury? It's possible due to very fast gas-producing chemical reaction to blow up the bag.

The Stone Age, the Iron Age and the Bronze Age are periods of history when humans began to exploit particular substances and so made massive improvements to their lives over a short period of time. It is oil, which has had the greatest impact on our lives. World supplies of oil are likely to run out before the end of the twenty-first century, but by then, other energy sources will have been developed. A possibility is hydrogen, derived from water. Hydrogen has several advantages: when it burns it produces no harmful products, it gives out more energy per gram than natural gas or petrol, and existing car engines need only minor modifications to use it as a fuel. Benzene is one of the most industrially important organic molecules. It features in the manufacture of petrochemicals, which are solvents, detergents, insecticides, dyes and polymers.

After a serious accident; such as a plane crash in a remote area, blood transfusions may have to be carried out under difficult conditions, but there may be time to identify and match a victim's blood group beforehand. Ideally, the rescue team needs a synthetic blood substitute that will suit all victims and do the vital job of carrying large amounts of Oxygen efficiently around the body. The blood substitute must also be inert and non-toxic and needs to be chemically stable.

You know that chemists investigate thousands of plants each year to see if they contain biologically active chemicals that might be developed into medical drugs. There is real hope that newly documented remedies will lead to drugs which treat cancer, heart disease and AIDS. The most publicized hormones must be progesterone and testosterone; the reason is sex. Progesterone is the female sex hormone, which prepares the uterus for pregnancy after an egg has been fertilized, and which prevents the ovaries from releasing any more eggs. Testosterone is the male sex hormone responsible for sexual development and drive in males, and for muscle growth; even a simple chemical reaction in the laboratory to convert progesterone to testosterone is perhaps no more striking example of the influence of chemistry on our lives.

First of all, 'think like a scientist'. When faced with a new experiment or problem, gather all the knowledge you already have about the subject, and list the data that is already 'given' or can be measured. This will help you develop an approach to solving the problem. Use this knowledge and review it if necessary. There is some memorization of facts involved in this book, though the key to success is understanding the principles.

☑ COMMON PROBLEMS FACED BY ALL STUDENTS:

- Often students sitting in a chemistry lecture fail to stop the teacher when they do not understand a problem or a concept. Ironically, many other students have the same question. Don't push it aside and hope that you will understand it later on; you are paying for the course, and you need to ask questions.
- Perhaps the most annoying situation a student gets into is working a problem out and failing to get the correct answer. This is not rare. Almost everyone works a problem wrong the first time. In addition, these mistakes teach us what we did wrong.
- "Which teacher should I take?" The teacher can make a big difference in your grade. Therefore, you should ask from senior students who have taken chemistry courses.
- "My teacher talks too fast and I can't keep up with

him while taking notes." The best thing to do in this situation is to bring a tape recorder into the lecture room and tape the lecture. Meanwhile, you can listen to the lecture and concentrate on any problems he or she may work on the board.

✓ STUDY TECHNIQUES FOR CHEMISTRY

Before taking any chemistry course, make sure that you have the required Mathematics skills. Since chemistry involves many calculations, regular attendance in class is essential. The classroom sessions are not meant to be lectures only, but times for discussion. Read the chapter before you go to class.

It is essential to keep up with the book, and there will be comprehensive techniques to simplify the subject. Please do not hesitate to ask questions, and take advantage of the school hours and of the tutorial service. We think you will find this book both interesting and useful. It will, however, require considerable time and energy to follow.

✓ TAKING PROBLEM-SOLVING TESTS:

- Before starting the test, turn it over and jot down all the formulas, relationships, definitions, etc. that you are trying to keep imprinted in your memory.
- Look the whole test over, skimming the questions and developing a general plan for your work. If any thoughts come to you immediately as you look at a problem, note these down in the margin.
- Plan your time. Allow more time for high point value problems; reserve time at the end of the period to review your work and for emergencies.
- Start with the easier problems, the ones for which you can specify a solution method quickly. This

will reduce anxiety and facilitate clear thinking.

ANALYZING PROBLEM SOLVING TESTS:

1. Read the comments and suggestions.
2. Locate the source of the test: did the problems come from the lectures, textbook, or homework?
3. Determine the source of your errors.
   - Were your errors due to carelessness?
   - Did you misread questions?
   - Could you produce the formulas, or did you remember them incorrectly?

BRAINWAVE: *Keep the gold and keep the silver, but give us wisdom.*

KEEP IN MIND: *Do everything you can to be a person of excellence now. It is your best preparation for future excellence.*

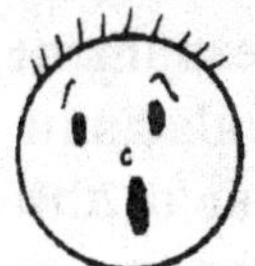

THINK ZONE: - *discovery, development, and application – will continue throughout …*

14

Measure Mathematics

Mathematics is the study of numbers, spatial relations and axiomatic systems. The branches of Mathematics under early investigation include arithmetic, geometry and algebra. Seventeenth century saw beginning of standard algebraic methods and introduction of calculus, probability most frequently applied Mathematical methods. Axiomatic development of Mathematics began in 19th century, which also saw perfection of techniques to solve classical problems. 20th century has seen grades subdivision of major areas of research, e.g. geometry now divided into topology, differentiated geometry, algebraic geometry, etc. as well

as development of abstract Mathematical system, originally arising out of specific problems, but now studied in their own right, as for group theory.

THE DEVELOPMENT OF MATHEMATICS

Mathematics is a subject that has a great many long-range objectives. One reason why mathematics enjoys special esteem, above all other sciences, is that its laws are absolutely certain and indisputable, while those of other sciences are to some extent debatable and in constant danger of being overthrown by newly discovered facts.

Many early civilizations, including the Egyptians, studied numbers as a science and recorded their discoveries. In India mathematics was largely centered on problems in astronomy. Negative and irrational numbers were used. Of course, India is noted for developing the concept of the *zero* that was passed into Western mathematics via the Arabic tradition, and is as important as a placeholder in our modern decimal number system. The two main sources of the current systems are the Greek philosopher, mathematician and astrologer, Pythagoras (called father of Numerology), born about 580 BC, and the Hebrew Kabbala, ancient Jewish tradition based on the Old Testament. Pythagoras suggested that the most powerful numbers were the odd, masculine numbers and the even, less powerful numbers were feminine. Algebra was developed only as far enough as to solve linear equations and, of course, calculate the volume of a pyramid. Johannes Kepler in 17th century linked music and mathematics and in 20th century Cheiro used numerology to predict general opinion.

The idea of a *point* as a pure location with no extension is an abstraction since a point cannot physically exist. A *dot* differs from a point in that a dot has extension, and represents only an approximate location. Nevertheless, since they can be seen, we use dots to represent points, which cannot be seen. Lines, planes and circles are also abstract ideas.

One of the most exciting advancements of the time was the introduction of Logarithms in 1614 by John Napier. However, the two big new ideas are Descartes' founding of analytic geometry, or geometry based on algebra, and the simultaneous but independent invention of calculus by Newton and Leibniz. With calculus at its center, an ever-widening body of knowledge began to take shape. The frontiers of mathematics in the eighteenth century included differential equations, infinite series, the study of planetary orbits, and the theory of numbers, solutions to algebraic equations, probability theory, and complex numbers.

Joseph Louis Lagrange (1736-1813) extended greatly our understanding of solutions to algebraic equations, and of planetary orbits. Another great French mathematician Pierre Simon de Laplace (1749-1827) made a major contribution in probability theory. Laplace treated mathematics as a tool whereas Lagrange considered mathematics as a thing of great beauty like poetry and created mathematics as an end in itself. Another important figure was D'Alembert (1717-1783), who did significant work in differential equations, sequences and series, mechanics, and astronomy.

Euler introduced many of today's familiar notations, including e, log x, sin x, cos x, f(x) for functions, and others. Non-Euclidean geometry is the study of geometries, which result from modifications of Euclid's axioms. Karl Pearson (1857-1936) founded statistics, as we know it today.

By the beginning of The Twentieth Century mathematics had grown wide and deep, so vast that it is impossible to summarize the subject here. Fly ahead to the twenty-first century, the rise of astrology to the advent of the nightly news, showing us how scientists and astrologers have attempted to predict the future. Will scientists ever be able to forecast catastrophes, or will we always be at the mercy of randomness, waiting for the next storm, epidemic, or economic crash to thunder through our lives?

MATHEMATICS IS ABOUT MASTERING A COLLECTION OF SKILLS

Mathematics is unlike other subjects. It has more to do with skills than knowledge and content. Mathematics is about mastering a collection of skills, and applying these skills to solve problems. It is important to understand fully what you are learning in Mathematics. Once you have understood a concept, it is important to practise various problems.

1. **Homework and study is not the same thing:** Homework is 'practise' work set by your teacher each day, reinforcing your learning of a particular skill. Study, on the other hand, is your own revision work for strengthening and improving your understanding of the subject.
2. **You cannot learn mathematics by halves you've got to know it all!** Unlike most subjects, all Mathematical knowledge is interconnected. This means the theory and skills of one Mathematics topic are related to those of another. Mathematics is also sequential, becoming more complex at each stage. You have to learn it in a particular order, so that if you miss out on an important step, then it becomes more difficult to progress. So

Mathematics is not a subject you can learn by halves. You must know it all in order to understand it properly.

3. **Mathematics question is often predictable...really!** However, once you have mastered your Mathematics skills that are it! You're done! You don't need to do any further reading or research to gain a deeper understanding of the subject. Compared to other subjects, the types of questions asked in Mathematics exams are more predictable and conventional, similar to the types of exercises you have seen in class.
4. **Practise your mathematics:** When you think you understand how to do a certain type of problem, you then need to practise doing it. The practise will not only help you understand and remember the work, but will also enable you to become so familiar with the work you can confidently, easily and fairly quickly work out that type of problem. When you practise, it is best to start with the easier examples. As with any type of skill, the only way of becoming a Mathematics master is by strengthening your abilities through practise, practise, and practise.
5. **Attack your mathematics:** Find your areas of weakness and work on them. Fill in any gaps in your Mathematical knowledge. Most of your study time should be spent on attacking your weaknesses. Use your topic summaries for general revision, but spend longer periods on in-depth work with your problem areas.
6. **Test your mathematics:** Finally test yourself using mixed revision exercises, assignments and past exams. After all, you are preparing for a big test

IITJEE, you need to go back and practise your Mathematics skill on a variety of questions. Studying past exam papers is an excellent way of adapting to the format of the questions and the level of difficulty expected. It will also help you to develop and improve your exam technique.

GETTING READY FOR YOUR MATHEMATICS FINAL

Here's a method of taking the sample exam that may point out your strengths and weaknesses to you, as well as get you the most points out of your final.

First, concentrate on classifying the problem, by identifying key symbols and phrases in the text of the problem, according to what techniques or theorems you would use to solve it, and make notes in the margins; also note how difficult you assess the problem to be.

Second, go through the exam and for each of the classifications made in the first step, solve the really easy problems and then the not-so-easy problems. What you'll be doing is warming up for the harder problems in each classification without constantly changing gears from one problem to the next, thus building momentum. Don't be afraid to make notes regarding where and why you got stuck on a problem. You may be reclassifying the problem, giving yourself the opportunity to get further through it as you do the problem of this new classification.

Third, go through the exam and check your solutions for accuracy and attempt to go ahead a little further with your partial solutions.

BRAINWAVE: *Mathematics is the queen mother of all the sciences.*

KEEP IN MIND: *Length of her days is in her right hand; and in her left hand riches and honour.*

THINK ZONE: *Death is not the greatest loss in life. The greatest loss is what dies inside us while we live.*

15

Paper Tactics

IIT-JEE CUT-OFFS LIKELY TO BE LOW THIS YEAR TOO

For all its reputation as one of the toughest competitive examinations in the world, IIT-JEE has seen a dramatic fall in standards. Under the new procedure for IIT-JEE, the cut-off is the highest scored by the bottom 20% of the candidates in each subject. But since such candidates are mostly non-serious, the cut-offs in mathematics, physics and chemistry worked out to no more than 1, 4 and 3, respectively. In 2006, the cutoff marks in maths, physics and chemistry were 37, 48 and 55 respectively. The reduction in cutoff marks to single digits has made a mockery of the concept which is meant to ensure that selected candidates display a certain minimum level of knowledge in each of the three subjects.

This has opened up the possibility of students making it to the merit list of IIT-JEE despite scoring nearly zero in the crucial test in mathematics.

IIT JOINT ENTRANCE EXAMINATION:

Neither underestimate yourself nor overestimate the IITJEE. The AIM of scripture is not to provide a recipe. It is to induce us to think for ourselves, to re-examine ourselves and our state of affairs.

MULTIPLE CHOICE QUESTIONS:

Before you even look at a question on a multiple-choice test, you must read the directions carefully. You must be sure of what is being asked of you. This cannot be stressed enough. You should begin each test by reading quickly through it once to answer the questions you are reasonably sure of. Mark those you can't answer so that you will be able to find them later. Go through the test a second time if you can't answer them. Begin each question by reading the stem all the way through. Then read the options all the way through. You should read all the options even when the question seems unfamiliar. One of them might provide you with a hint as to what the question is about. There might be information in the options themselves. If you cannot answer it quickly, cross out any options you have eliminated and go on to return later to the question. Your job is to pick the alternative that is more nearly true than the others are. Read multiple-choice questions the same way as for true false. Eliminate obvious false choices; Learn to spot the key words in the statement that defines the meaning. If you cannot eliminate all options to a question you should guess when there is no penalty for guessing.

STEPS TO TAKE MULTIPLE CHOICE QUESTIONS:

In IIT-JEE there is thorough testing of the subject knowledge and problem solving skills of the candidate. Thus the only requirement of this examination is to have strong basic concepts, good analytical skills, and thorough knowledge of the subject matter and rigorous practise of questions.

1. Survey the Test: Survey any objective examination to find out what types of questions are being asked. Glance at all the pages.

- How long is it?
- Are you missing any pages?
- What types of questions are there?

2. Write out any memorized lists onto the exam sheet. At the top of the paper write the halfway time and the halfway question number. The multiple-choice questions, matching, and true-false question have at least one thing in common - the correct answer is provided. Your problem as a test taker is to identify it.

3. Read the directions carefully. Always read directions! Indicate your answers exactly the way the directions state. Make sure your answers are clear. Determine what the scoring rules for the test are and follow them to your advantage. For example, if wrong answers are penalized, don't guess unless you can reduce the choices to two.

- Is there a penalty for guessing? (If not, answer all the questions.)
- Are all the questions weighted equally?
- For multiple choices: Is there only ONE correct choice for each question?

4. Answering easy (to you) questions first, is the best strategy.

- Cross out both negatives of a double negative.
- Underline dogmatic terms. Statements containing them are usually false because few things in the world meet the requirements of 'always, never, best, etc.'
- True - False. Be careful of statements with two clauses.
- Matching: Read all items before making any matches.

5. Checking your answers.

- All questions are answered (if no penalty for guessing).
- All choices are clearly marked.
- All 'X's' and '?'S' on the answer sheet has been erased.

6. Rework all questions if you have time.

- First, work on unanswered questions with 'X'.
- Second, rework questions with a '?'.
- Third, reword the rest of the questions.

7. Always try to guess what the answer is before you look at the choices. Try to remember if any of the answers left are related to that subject. Do you remember seeing that word in the chapter?

8. All-of-the-above questions: If 2 or more of the answers are correct, then the all-of-the-above option is the correct answer, EVEN IF you are unsure of the third option.

9. Look-alike options: Sometimes there are 2 options that are alike except for one word. Such a pair indicates that the question is focused there. USUALLY, not always, you can assume the answer is one of that pair.

HOW TO ANSWER SUBJECTIVE QUESTIONS:

CBSE test papers to turn brainy: Class X and XII 10% of paper will comprise very-short answer questions, 20% will be designed to assess HOTS (High Order Thinking Skills). Planning your time in answering subjective questions is more important than in objective type tests. The general rule is not to get carried away on one or two questions to the extent that you cannot answer other questions in the time allowed.

COUNTER TO SOME KEY WORDS

- **Comment** - discuss briefly
- **Compare** - emphasize similarities and differences
- **Define** - give meaning but no details
- **Discuss** - give reasons pros and cons, with details
- **Explain** - give reasons for happenings or situations
- **Give an example** - give a concrete example
- **Justify** - prove or give reasons
- **Solve** - come up with a solution based on given facts

STEPS TO WRITE SUBJECTIVE QUESTIONS:

You must determine the exact idea that the teacher is trying to get at. A good plan before you start writing will save your time. These steps are not meant to tell you what to write but rather how to compose and word your answers.

- **Read the examination directions carefully; read all the questions:** Before you write anything, read all the questions. If you have a choice among questions, select those for which you are best prepared.
- **Jot cues alongside each question; plan your time:** While reading each question, quickly note a few words or phrases that immediately come to your mind. Later, when you begin writing, use these

jottings and those on the back of the exam sheet to organize your answer; then decide how much time to give each question, and stick to your plan.

- **Start with the easiest question; strive for a complete answer:** Don't sit and stare at the first exam question. Seize on an easy one, number the answer correctly, and start writing. State your ideas explicitly. Do not leave anything to be inferred or concluded by the teacher. Show the complete process of your thinking.
- **Use facts and logic, not vague impressions or feelings:** Teachers are not interested in your personal likes or dislikes, emotions, attitude or feelings. They are concerned with how well you understand the material.
- **Be concise; organize your answer intelligently:** The most impressive answer is invariably presented in a direct and straightforward manner. Focus on either one central idea, or several main points.

To reach at top follow opportunities that are born out of adversity. When things are going well, everybody does well. But when everything is going well for everybody, you have to ask yourself: what makes you different, what distinguishes you from the rest?

FIND STRENGTH IN YOUR WEAKNESS

A water bearer in India had two large pots, each hung on the end of a pole which he carried across his neck. One of the pots was perfectly made and never leaked. The other pot had a crack in it and by the time the water bearer reached his master's house it had leaked much of it's water and was only half full.

For a full two years this went on daily, with the bearer delivering only one and a half pots full of water to his master's house. Of course, the perfect pot was proud of its accomplishments. But the poor cracked pot was ashamed of its own imperfection, and miserable that it was able to accomplish only half of what it had been made to do.

After two years of what it perceived to be a bitter failure, it spoke to the water bearer one day by the stream. "I am ashamed of myself, and I want to apologize to you." "Why?" asked the bearer? "What are you ashamed of?" "I have been able, for these past two years, to deliver only half my load because this crack in my side causes water to leak out all the way back to your master's house. Because of my flaws, you have to do all of this work, and you don't get full value from your efforts," the pot said.

The water bearer felt sorry for the old cracked pot, and in his compassion he said, "As we return to the master's house, I want you to notice the beautiful flowers along the path."

Indeed, as they went up the hill, the old cracked pot took notice of the sun warming the beautiful wild flowers on the side of the path, and this cheered it a little. But at the end of the trail, it still felt bad because it had leaked out half its load, and so again the pot apologized to the bearer for its failure.

The bearer said to the pot, "Did you notice that there were flowers only on your side of your path, but not on the other pot's side? That's because I have always known about your flaw, and I took advantage of it. I planted flower seeds on your side of the path, and every day while we walk back from the stream, you've watered them. For two years I have been able to pick these beautiful flowers to decorate my master's table. Without you being just the way you are, he would not have this beauty to grace his house."

Each of us has our own unique flaws. We're all cracked pots. But if we will allow it, God will use our flaws to grace his table. In God's great economy, nothing goes to waste. Don't be afraid of your flaws. Acknowledge them, and you too can be the cause of beauty. Know that in our weakness we find our strength.

BRAINWAVE: *Let everyone sweep in front of their door and the whole world will be clean.*

KEEP IN MIND: *Remember who you are, she said. You're a master.*

THINK ZONE: *Delete what needs to be eliminated from life – you will feel lighter, happier and your mind will experience more peace.*

16

JEE Psychoanalysis

☑ OPEN EXAM PROCESS TO STUDENTS

Results of the IIT's Joint Entrance Examination (IIT-JEE), one of the most keenly contested examinations in the country, just got more transparent. IIT Joint Admission Board has decided to release the cut-off scores in individual subjects like physics, maths or chemistry and also aggregate cut-offs for stream like computer, electronics, mechanical and civil engineering. The score sheets will be displayed the opening and closing ranks of different branches for every category, general and reserved.

☑ IITJEE DREAM THERAPY

The Indian Institutes of Technologies (IITs) have

received world wide recognition for their standards of excellence and have been producing technological manpower for development and carrying out many research programs.

In JEE about 3 lakh candidates appear, it can be easily inferred that the majority of them (about 75%) are not having a preparation that can make it to the IITs. Most of them dream of getting into IIT as soon as they complete there class X board examinations, buy a lot of study material, and instead of studying, continue to dream for the next 2 years and in the end they wait for a miracle to happen and finally fail to qualify.

Out of the remaining 60,000 candidates, 40,000 aspirants who try hard for the exam but in the end cannot reach the desired level of JEE. The final 20,000 candidates are the actual competitors for JEE. They work hard through close up out the two years and appear in the JEE with full confidence.

It is common among all the students to practise an enormous number of multiple choice questions (MCQ) throughout the year. This is however a wrong way; because, the multiple choice questions those are given in most of the study materials and magazines do not reflect the exact nature of the Paper. You should keep away from doing this kind of practise. JEE demands clarity of each and every concept. One month before the JEE, revise each and every formula you know, so that if you are not clear with the concept you can still reach the answer with a derived formula. Also get a few good practise screening papers and attempt those tests under strict examination conditions. This actually helps you learn the aspects of time management.

The key to success in JEE is extensive practise of subjective problems. You will have to excel yourself at pattern recognition along with developing the concepts.

Please do not go in for absurd problems as they are never asked in JEE. Also JEE problems do not require a very long solution.

JEE papers which were once dreaded as the toughest papers set for the school level, consisting of incomprehensible questions, seem to be undergoing some reform as the questions have been simplified. Questions now demand only basic concepts and no problems require advance level knowledge. JEE can now be cleared by studying the school level books.

IITJEE ANALYSIS

Firstly, it is important to recognize the requirement of the exam. Most of the questions asked require you to probe and work out the solution. Even the paper-setters do not expect the students to answer all the questions correctly in the time allotted. The proof of this lies in the fact, that never in the recent history of the exam have the minimum qualifying marks been more than 30-35 per cent. Therefore, logically, if you can score even 40% marks in each paper; you can obtain a good rank.

The IIT-JEE examination is conducted to identify the aspirants who have the potential to play a vital role in developing technologies in the future. Analysis of previous year's papers will enable a candidate to assess and comprehend the analytical and reasoning skills required to tackle IIT-JEE problems. The strategy based on this comprehension guarantees a good rank in the IIT-JEE merit list.

Analyzing the nature of questions which had appeared in the previous years. IIT-JEE papers will help the students understand the pattern of questions in the IIT-JEE. The professors who set the papers at IIT-JEE have a tough job at hand: they have to set the paper in such a way as to be able to shortlist about seven thousand students from about more than three lac candidates that is just two and half per cent who will be admitted in to those hallowed portals. This is accomplished by designing questions that do not aim to test how well informed the student is, but to determine the depth of his knowledge. The JEE paper is a balanced paper of three subjects Physics, Chemistry and Mathematics. There are number of sets of question paper each containing the same questions in different order. The JEE shift has been towards the core CBSE concepts. This indicates that the most important requirement for success at the JEE is the ability to understand clearly the core of the subjects.

BLUEPRINT OF IITJEE

1. This was the traditional multiple choice question pattern with one correct option. The questions were elementary and the skill required would be to simply understand the question, find the answer and pick that from among the choices.

2. What was needed was the ability to link two different statements and, as a doctor would do, decide on cause and effect.

The skill required was to understand the real links between concepts, that is, the *why* and *how* of the linkages.

3. This tested the analytical ability of students some questions were of the type where problem described had to be solved on the basis of the given information. It was similar to the reading comprehension-type questions.

The difference is, the student had to bring in the knowledge acquired in the concerned subject, and not just answer on the basis of the passage. The questions were also interlinked in some cases.

4. How many roads lead from City A to City B? And from City C to city D?

Getting from one point to another was not the issue

here. You needed to know all the paths. The skill required complete mastery of the topography. That is what this section of questions also sought in the students.

FINAL SEGMENT

It is time to give you a clear insight into the relationship between preparing for the exam and succeeding in it. According to the findings of our panel of experts, apart from starting as early as 2 years in advance and putting in 3 to 5 hours of study everyday, the successful students devote at least 4 to 6 weeks before the exams getting familiar with the latest and contemporary problems. This is the secret of their success. Let us assume that after the class XII exam, you get about two weeks for the IIT-JEE and that you can put in 8-10 hours of productive study each day. You get a total of, say 135 hours, which translates into 45 hours per subject.

This is too short a period to even glance through all the topics of the subject. So do not even attempt to complete the syllabus. Fortunately, you are not expected to. Aim to master around 60 per cent of the syllabus. This is for those students who have been out of touch with JEE for, say the past five or six months. However, for those who have been putting in a steady number of hours, it is possible to complete 80 per cent of the syllabus.

What should you study and what should you leave out? That's simple. Every subject contains some topics that are either difficult to comprehend or that require more time to develop an intuitive insight into in order to understand the underlying difficulty in apparently simple forms. Friction, rotational motion, fluid motion, wave mechanics, volumetric analysis, ionic equilibrium, hybridization, heights and distances, combinations, inequalities, induction, binomial coefficients are some such topics.

If you aren't comfortable with them avoid them for the present. However if you are comfortable tackling such topics, do include them. They carry a good 12-20 per cent of the total marks. Remember: what is learnt with pleasure is learnt in full measure. As for the easier topics, there's only one way out: master them. These get included in the 60 per cent that you master.

The right reference material makes a big difference. As coaching classes are in vogue, students can avail of this facility as well. However, take assistance from those teachers who specialize in analyzing instead of just solving problems. Here is a suggested list of topics that you should master:

☑ **PHYSICS:** In Physics some of the problems are presented graphically and most of the questions require calculation for getting the answer. The problems are presented in both verbal and diagrammatic forms and solutions are required in both numerical and graphic form. One must therefore, remember that there is no particular pattern of problem and solution presentation. One has therefore to use analytical and reasoning skills in addition to implementing the concepts of physics.

The topics you should master are: Thermodynamics, Conduction and Convection of Heat, Hydrostatics and Bernoulli's Principle, Waves in Elastic Media, Interference Beats and Doppler's Effect, Electrostatics (full), Electromagnetic Induction, Lorentz' Forces, Circuits with Capacitors, Modern Physics (full), Collisions, Rotational Motion, Gravitation, Elasticity, S.H.M.

The approximate weight age of topics in JEE:

- Mechanics 30%
- Fluid Mechanics 08%
- Waves 07%
- Heat & Thermodynamics 05%

- Optics 10%
- Electrostatics & Electricity 10%
- Magnetism & Magnetic Effects of currents 05%
- EMI, AC Circuits and DC Source 05%
- Modern Physics 10%
- Miscellaneous 10%

☑ **CHEMISTRY:** In Chemistry the emphasis is on verbal presentation of problems. Except for a few questions, calculation is not required for getting the answer. Some questions are reasoning-based. Conceptual questions are the backbone of the section on chemistry. Few questions are conceptual in organic chemistry; most of the questions require a basic understanding of the topics.

The topics you should master are: Atomic structure, Bonding, Redox Reactions, Volumetric analysis, Chemical Equilibrium and Kinetics, Ionic Equilibrium, Electrochemical Cells, Solutions, Hess's Law, Organic Chemistry (full) with special stress on reaction mechanism of reactions named in the syllabus, Oxyacids of P,S, C & N, Properties of Ozone Thiosulphates, Hydrogen peroxide, Coordination Compounds.

The approximate weight age of topics in JEE:

- Physical Chemistry 35%
- Organic Chemistry 30%
- Inorganic Chemistry 30%
- Miscellaneous 05%

☑ **MATHEMATICS:** The physics paper has been comparatively easier, whereas the Mathematics paper has traditionally remained tough. The mathematical concepts are required. Most of the problems involve a lot of calculation and are time consuming. Among the three sections, this is accepted as the most difficult section.

The topics you should master are: Calculus (full), Quadratic Equations and Expressions, Complex Numbers, Progressions, Solution of Triangles, Solution of Trigonometric Equations, Vector Analysis, Straight Lines, either Circles or Conic section.

The approximate weight age of topics in JEE:

- Algebra 25%
- Trigonometry 05%
- Two Dimensional Geometry 20%
- Calculus 25%
- Miscellaneous 25%

BRAINWAVE: *When I look back on all these worries I remember the story of the old man who said on his deathbed that he had had a lot of trouble in his life, most of which never happened.*

KEEP IN MIND: *Inspect every piece of pseudo-science and you will find a security blanket, a thumb to suck, a skirt to hold. What have we to offer in exchange? Uncertainty! Insecurity!*

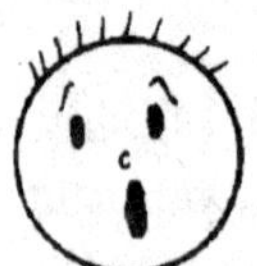

THINK ZONE: *They chose their paths not because they were easy, but because they were difficult.*

```
P R O B L E M H T I R A G O L
R E E D D I V I D E I L P P A
O V Q S T A T I S T I C S E T
D E U U S U B T R A C T N R O
U N A L A V E C T O R H O A T
C P L U U T O O R I E E I N U
T A G C D H I M G C M O T D S
G R E L E D E O I T A R C I L
E A B A C D N G N D I E A D O
O M R C I O O S D P N M R I P
M E A A M L S U M O D E F G E
E T N E A E W R E G E T N I G
T E T T L U S E R O R R E T N
R R Y L P I T L U M O R E G A
Y T L I B A B O R P D N U O R
```

ADD
ALGEBRA
APPLIED
CALCULUS
DECIMAL
DIGIT
DIVIDE
EQUAL
EQUATION
ERROR
EVEN
FRACTION
GEOMETRY
INTEGER
LESS
LOGARITHM
LOGIC
MEDIAN
MODE
MORE
MULTIPLY
ODD
OPERAND
PARAMETER
PI
PROBABILTY
PROBLEM
PRODUCT
RANGE
RATIO
REMAINDER
RESULT
ROOT
ROUND
SLOPE
STATISTICS
SUBTRACT
SUM
THEOREM
TOTAL
TRIGONOMETRY
VECTOR

17
Exam Anxiety

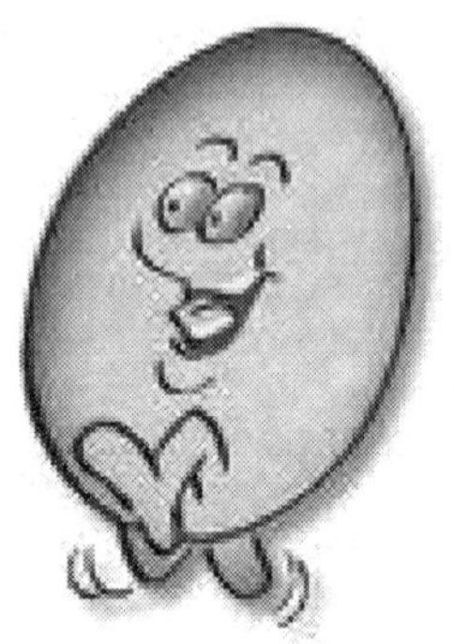

WHAT IS EXAM ANXIETY?

Anxiety is a natural part of competition at any age level. Exam is a word that brings fear. No matter how many exams you may have taken, there is always a certain amount of stress associated with them. Exam anxiety is usually a result of not being prepared. Exam anxiety is also associated with a fear of failing. Anxiety can either enhance or inhibit performance. "Exam anxiety is not a fear of tests. It is a fear created from not being prepared."

Preparing for and writing exams are among the most important and stressful aspects of student life. A certain amount of test anxiety is normal. It can actually improve your academic performance by helping you concentrate on the task at hand and stay motivated and alert. Some students experience more severe anxiety that can be counterproductive. Research has demonstrated that highly anxious students tend to receive lower scores in exams than do less anxious students, even when ability and preparation are the same. Anxiety always lies in between fear and hope.

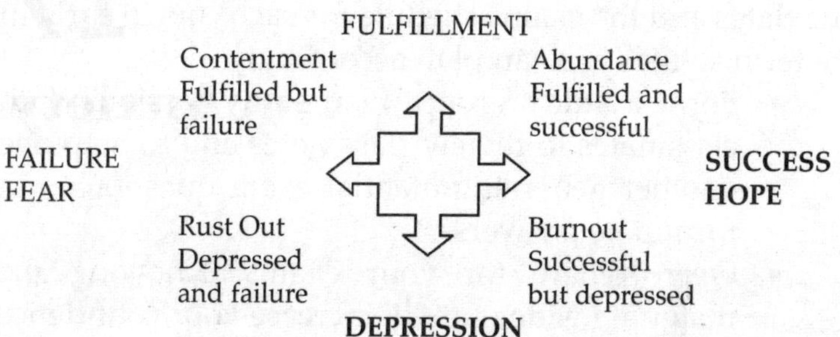

SYMPTOMS OF EXAM ANXIETY

Many students describe experiencing some of the following symptoms of anxiety before or during an exam. Some students confuse the symptoms and consequences of exam anxiety with other learning and attention problems. If you do have difficulties with learning and/or attention, you may be more likely to experience anxiety during exam preparation and the writing of exams.

PHYSICAL	BEHAVIOURAL	EMOTIONAL
Fatigue	Disturbed sleep	Stress
Chest pain	Not attending class	Worry
Headache	Procrastination	Irritability
Upset stomach	Increased alcohol use	Frustration
Muscle tension	Increased caffeine use	Confusion
Rapid heart rate	Distractibility	Disorientation
Lightheadedness	Restlessness	Feeling of being overwhelmed

WAYS TO MANAGE EXAM ANXIETY

The best way to do well in any test is to be prepared. There are no exceptions to this rule. No technique will help if you do not know the material. Do what you can, with what you have, where you are. Success is simple. Do what's right, the right way, at the right time. Determine due dates and the exam schedule for each course early in the term so that you can plan accordingly.

- Form a study group. Plan study sessions with classmates to review class notes and to help one another generate potential exam questions and formulate answers.
- Over-prepare for your exams. Knowing the material inside out will increase your confidence and help reduce anxiety. For this technique to be successful you need to organize your schedule so you have ample time to prepare.
- Gather the supplies you will need for your exam. Don't wait until the last minute to look for your calculator or ruler. The less you have to worry about prior to the exam, the better.
- Get a good night's rest before the exam. For most students, this is essential to good exam performance.
- Be on time. Rushing to an exam or arriving late will increase your anxiety. You should double-check the exam time and location well in advance.
- Be aware of your thinking. Are you telling yourself "I'm going to fail," "I always blank out during exams," or do you say, "I can write this exam," "I am going to stay calm"? Positive thinking can help you respond to stressful situations more effectively.
- Focus on the present. Try to avoid thinking about

past or future exams. Try not to pay attention to what other students are doing.

- Take the time to read exam questions carefully. Answer questions you are sure of, before you attempt more difficult ones. This builds confidence and gives you a sense of accomplishment.
- After finishing an exam double-check your answers. After writing an exam, evaluate your effort. Notice any areas of difficulty. Acknowledge your successes and willingness to improve your skills.

INSOMNIA CAN BE STOPPED

Sleep serves a restorative function for the body and the brain. It is important for daily functioning, as it can influence health, mood, behaviour, relationships, work and school performance. There are differences in the amount of sleep people require. A good night's sleep can range from several hours for some people, to more than ten hours for others. Insomnia occurs when individuals have difficulty falling or staying asleep, or do not feel refreshed by the amount of sleep they get. It is associated with feelings of distress, fatigue and/or reduced performance during the day.

CAUSES OF INSOMNIA

Remember that it is normal to experience short-term problems with sleep during times of excitement, when feeling stressed or worried. Many factors can contribute to the development of insomnia, including:

- Poor sleeping habits (e.g. not maintaining a regular sleep-waking up schedule) and lifestyle patterns (e.g. diet and lack of exercise).

• Psychological problems and chronic stress (e.g. relationship problems, on-going academic concerns).

• Medical conditions (e.g. allergies, chronic back pain, hormonal changes).

☑ WAYS TO MANAGE INSOMNIA

While there is no single treatment for insomnia, some of the suggestions listed below may be helpful. Consult your family doctor if your insomnia is persistent and interferes with your daily life.

- Establish a regular sleep-waking up schedule. (i.e. Have a fixed time to go to bed and particularly to get up in the morning), Maintain a comfortable sleep environment. Many people find that a dark, quiet bedroom is conducive to good sleep. Try to minimize sleep interruptions.
- Try to avoid large, heavy dinners late in the evening, and snacks that may give you heartburn or indigestion. Try to eat nutritious meals. People who lack proper nutrients in their diet may experience insomnia. Avoid excessive use of caffeine. Even as little as two cups of coffee or two cola drinks consumed in a day can interfere with sleep.
- Exercise on a regular basis. Twenty to thirty minutes of exercise, several times per week may help promote sleep. Remember that sleep-related problems can be related to a mood disturbance such as depression or anxiety. If you feel this is your situation, contact a psychiatrist.

☑ THE FIFTEEN-MINUTE DRILL

With your talents and approach the industry with science, and steadfast honesty, which eternally pursues right, regardless of consequences, you may promise yourself everything but prime is health, without which there is no happiness. Nothing is more consistently prescribed by physicians for a healthy, energetic, and productive life than exercise. You can achieve these goals for yourself.

A man dies at night daily, only to be reborn in the morning, bigger, better, and wiser. We live incredibly hectic lives, doing more with less and less. You can defeat the resulting stress before it gets you. After lying in bed for fifteen minutes without falling asleep, get up and do something relaxing. Then return to sleep again.

RELAXATION

Relaxation is a human need – physically, mentally and spiritually. Recognize some of the body's signals of tension and upset feelings. Turn inward to see your happy face, or listen inwardly to a word or sound that can help in stressful situations. Slowly take a deep breath, and slowly breathe out. Sense the tense air going out, and the calm air coming in.

EXERCISE

Physical exercise is an excellent way to rid the body of the effects of stress. Exercise dissipates the effects of stress and helps the body return to normal. It lessens anxiety and depression, and affords a sense of calm and well-being.

RECREATION

Everyone should arrange a daily schedule of play. It should be considered a natural good-health practise. It provides diversion for the mind and lets it change its focus from problems to a chosen, personally satisfying, activity.

EXPRESS YOUR FEELINGS

Probably the most significant way to release tension is to talk one's feelings over with someone else. A very direct statement of one's feelings can be very helpful. The other person hears them and acknowledges them. Sometimes that is all that is needed. Drawing pictures representing these feelings or maintaining a journal or diary to jot down your thoughts and feelings also be helpful.

BRAINWAVE: *Anxiety always lies in between fear and hope.*

KEEP IN MIND: *You can't win a game that you don't even play.*

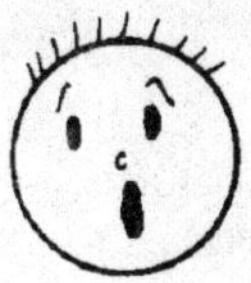

THINK ZONE: *Real risk lies in risk less living.*

18

JEE Count Down

☑ THE FINAL RUN-UP TO THE EXAMS:

If you stick to your study timetable, you should be able to avoid the sweating in the last few days. But for most people it is sensible to try at least to reduce the intensity of their studying and to get some thorough relaxation as the countdown begins. Avoid discussing the exam that is to commence shortly with your classmates as you mill about outside the exam hall waiting to enter. Likewise, avoid discussing the paper immediately after an exam, if you have another exam coming up soon afterwards. Don't engage in 'post-mortems' with your classmates or even with yourself as such discussions tend to be demoralizing rather than reassuring, and save only to distract you from preparing for the exam ahead.

SIX DAY COUNTDOWN FOR AN EXAM

Time is the most valuable resource a student has. It is also one of the most wasted of all resources. The schedule you develop should determine how you allocate the available time in the most productive manner. Sticking to your schedule can be tough. Don't dribble away valuable time. **Avoiding study is the easiest thing in the world**. It's up to you to follow the schedule you prepared. A good deal of your success in IITJEE depends on this simple truth.

The Most Valuable Commodity In The World Is Time; Like An Arrow Shot From A Bow, It Never Returns.

The ideal test preparation model is to study and read ahead of the exam. Yet if you have to cram well it is best to use a systematic, controlled method. First of all you have to be realistic about what you can learn and thus distill the material into a workable amount. Remember, cramming cannot and will not be as effective as conscientious studying from well before the exam. The countdown days can be altered to fit your situation. It might seem like there is a mountain of information containing the unusual and the unknown; the task may seem impossible but with a well chalked out plan. It is EASY.

BEFORE THE COUNTDOWN

Let us breakdown the time day-wise. There should be about 3-4 MAIN ideas. Review your notes and encircle anything you don't understand. Look them up in the book.

SIXTH DAY BEFORE THE EXAM: ASSESSMENT

- What portion will be covered in the test? Is it a cumulative test or not? What material am I responsible for?

- Have I read all the material? If not, it is probably too late to read all the material. If you have completed nearly all the material, go ahead and finish it.
- What are the main topics of testable material? What might the teacher stress in the test? A review of your lecture notes and the themes the teacher concentrated upon or spent a great deal of time on are good indicators of the likely topics of the test.
- Do I understand the material? If the material is understood, it is more easily remembered. If you do not understand something, you should ask your teacher/friend to explain.
- What type of memory work will be stressed? You may be asked to recall information (essay type) or simply recognize the correct answer (objective type).

☑ FIFTH DAY BEFORE THE EXAM

Decide how much more background information you need or can learn within the time limit before the test. This is an important and critical step, for you might have to eliminate certain material in order to limit the material to a workable amount. At this point you may need to 'take your chances' and make an educated guess on what will and will not be in the test, then only study those topics you believe will be on the exam.

☑ FOURTH DAY BEFORE EXAM

- Have you outlined the material? You should write a general outline of a page or two, stressing the highlights and main points of the material. It will be easier for you to remember an organized outline than a disorganized set of notes.

- Does your outline capture the major portion of the material that needs to be known for the test?

THIRD DAY BEFORE THE EXAM

Quiz yourself or test yourself with a friend on yesterday's material. This is the crucial step for this is the actual 'cramming' stage. It is here that you are attempting to stuff the material into your head.

- Have you studied the items you need to remember the most? The items that you study first will be remembered more accurately and for a longer period of time.
- Are you learning complete sections at a time? It is likely that you will be asked to recall a complete section of material at a single time in the exam, so it is best to memorize the material in entire outline sections.
- Are you able to make a mental impression of the material? If you can see the outline in your mind, it will make the memorization process much more effective and your knowledge of the material much more complete. Form a 'cheat sheet' in your mind, if you will.

Can you form your own examples, applications and illustrations of the material? This is not applicable to all of the material. If you can make your own illustrations explaining the material, it is usually a sign that you have a good grasp of the material.

SECOND DAY BEFORE THE EXAM

Do a test again today. Test yourself on the whole chapter. A good thing to do is to get together with a friend for a question-and-answer session. The night before the test may not be a good time to do this because the other person may hinder your progress or not concentrate on what YOU need to know (when you teach a friend you learn a lot). Highlight in your notes what you still do not know or are unsure of.

ONE DAY BEFORE THE EXAM: REVIEW

A day before the exam make sure you have rehearsed the material. Once you have learned the various sections of material, go over it all together a couple of times.

Make a list of all the highlighted information you still don't know. Study those and the little details you may have overlooked before. By now you should know everything like the back of your hand. Sleep early enough so you will wake up refreshed in the morning. If you do not get enough sleep the night before the exam, you will forget more than you might have learned otherwise. Go to bed early.

ON THE EXAMINATION DAY

Get up early enough to review the material once before the exam. Reviewing the material on the morning of the exam will keep it fresh in your mind. Do not attempt to study immediately before the test. Studying immediately before the exam will more likely create confusion in your mind about the material.

PREPARATION PRIOR TO THE EXAMINATION

- Have a light meal before the examination. Avoid a large, heavy meal; it might make you drowsy.
- Dress comfortably on the day of the exam; avoid tight-fitting clothing.

- Get a good night's sleep before the examination; avoid the use of stimulants.
- You should bring at least two pens, two soft-lead (HB) pencils, a good eraser and other required stationery well in advance for the test.
- Arrive well in advance for the exam.
- Bring your admission letter.

☑ DURING THE EXAMINATION

Bring a watch and put it in a convenient location on the desk. Pace yourself: set the average time per question. Do not spend a long time on a simple question. If you are unsure of an answer, mark what you believe to be the correct answer on your answer sheet; you may wish to circle the item in the test book and return to reconsider it later if you have extra time. Set up checkpoints during the examination to determine how well you are pacing yourself. If you do not have a clue to the correct answer for a particular question, skip it, and return to it later. When you return to the question if you still have no clue, remember that no one knows all the answers.

GOOD LUCK!

☑ AFTER COMPLETING THE EXAMINATION

Evaluate your work. Complete the following statement and list as many reasons as fit the statement:

Tests scare me because:

____

____

There are many excuses for not doing well in an exam. Usually the main reason students do not do well in a test is that they are not well prepared.

BRAINWAVE: *Before you start a test close your eyes, take a deep breath, relax and don't Panic. If you care enough for the result, you will almost always attain it.*

KEEP IN MIND: *You may forget the one with whom you have laughed. But never the one with whom you have wept.*

THINK ZONE: *When you reach your height you shall desire but only for desire; and you shall hunger, for hunger; and you shall thirst for greater thirst.*

19

Introduction IIT

SCIENTIFIC HERITAGE OF INDIA

"Science education should... emphasize life learning and life skills. The perceived relevance of scientific process and context to everyday life experiences is a factor in science interest and participation at both the pre-college and collegiate levels."

A vast number of individuals have contributed to the rich scientific heritage of India. People like Alberuni, though an Arabian worked extensively in India to introduce a new paradigm of experimentation to scientific investigation during the middle Ages in his relentless pursuit of truth. Modern researchers like C.V. Raman, who won the Noble Prize for his work in physics in the 1920s, established India as a respected international player in a highly competitive research environment.

In a society where science and culture are so intimately woven together, politicians such as Jawaharal Nehru played a significant role in the establishment of educational and governmental programs and institutions that have given science a place of respected priority among a people with a long tradition of scientific inquiry. The IIT is an educational institute where your personality will be groomed to an international level. In the corporate world, at the global level at least one and at national level four among the top ten would be an IITian; and 20 per cents of those in the Silicon Valley are IITians.

INTRODUCTION: IIT

The Indian Institutes of Technology are institutions of national importance established through an act of Parliament. These institutes play a leading role in technological manpower development and research programmes comparable to the best in the world. The admissions to the undergraduate programmes for all Indian and foreign nationals at these institutions are made through the Joint Entrance Examination (JEE). The institute of Technology—Banaras Hindu University, Varanasi is one of the oldest institutions devoted to education in various engineering disciplines. Indian School of Mines, Dhanbad, a deemed university, is likewise the oldest institution of its kind in India. The admissions to the Undergraduate Programmes at these institutions are also made through the JEE. These institutions are known for providing quality technological and scientific education and for research in frontier areas. The environment at all these institutions is highly conducive for:

- Building of solid foundation of knowledge,
- Development of personality,

- Confidence building,
- Enhancement of creativity through motivation and drive, which helps to produce professionals well trained for the rigours of professional and social life.
- Pursuit of excellence and self-discipline,

India's exclusive engineering club has been expanded; The Union HRD ministry has decided to open six new IITs instead of just the three which were supposed to begin operations this year in Bihar, Rajasthan and Andhra Pradesh; three more in Orissa, Punjab and Gujarat as well from this year. There will now be 13 IITs with a total of 6,872 seats. More than 700 seats have been added thanks to the six new IITs. Each IIT will have 120 seats and three courses will be offered in the first year. Classes for IITs in Punjab, Orissa and Rajasthan will function out of the IITs in Delhi, Kanpur and Kharagpur respectively, according to officials. Two more IITs—in Himachal Pradesh and Madhya Pradesh—are slated to start next year.

These institutes offer courses leading to Bachelor's degree in a number of engineering, technological and scientific disciplines. In addition, some IITs offer dual-degree M.Tech. programmes, wherein both B.Tech. and M.Tech. Degrees are awarded at the end of the programme.

JEE SCHEDULE

It is held on the second Sunday of April.

- 0900 -1200 hrs. Paper-1
- 1400-1700 hrs. Paper-2

ELIGIBILITY:

A candidate can attempt JEE only twice, in consecutive years. Candidates who have passed (10+2) or equivalent qualifying examination in last year or will be appearing in current year, and secure 60% or more [55% or more for SC/ST and persons with Physical Disability (PD)] marks in aggregate in their respective Board Examination are eligible. If any Board awards only letter-grades, the candidate should obtain a certificate from the Board specifying equivalent percentage marks. In case the respective Board awards letter-grades without providing norms for converting them to equivalent percentage marks, the norms decided by the Joint Implementation Committee, JEE shall be final.

PATTERN OF EXAMINATION

The examination will consist of two papers, each of three hours duration. Paper-1 and Paper-2 will each have three separate sections on Physics, Chemistry and Mathematics. Both papers will be of objective type, designed to test comprehension, reasoning and analytical ability of candidates. Aptitude tests for B.Arch and B.Des. programmes will be conducted for those candidates who qualify in JEE and are desirous of joining these programmes. The syllabus is available on the websites of all IITs and in the Information Brochure. Use of calculators and log tables are NOT permitted in **JEE**.

Language for Question Papers

English / Hindi

Aptitude Test for B.Arch. and B.Des.

Candidates called for counselling and desirous of joining the B.Arch. and B.Des. courses will be required to qualify in an Aptitude Test to be conducted at each counselling institute in June. The test will consist of two papers, each of two hours duration – from 10.00 a.m. to 12.00 noon, and from 2.00 pm to 4:00 pm. Candidates who fail to qualify in the Aptitude Test will not be eligible for admission to B.Arch / B.Des. courses. The question papers for aptitude test for B.Arch. and B.Des. will be in English only.

RANKING

Only those candidates who attempt both Paper 1 and Paper 2 will be considered for the ranking. Marks in Physics will be equal to marks in Physics section of Paper 1 + marks in Physics section of Paper 2. Similar procedure will be followed for Chemistry and Mathematics. Based on the cut-off marks in the individual subjects as well as the aggregate marks in the Examination, a common merit list will be prepared without any relaxation criteria. In addition, separate merit lists of candidates belonging to the SC, ST, and PD categories will be prepared with different relaxed norms relevant to their categories. While preparing these merit lists, if a candidate belongs to more than one category of relaxed norms, then he/she for the purpose of ranking shall be considered in all the categories in which he/she qualifies. There will be no separate list of wait-listed candidates.

CONTACT INFORMATION

Institute IIT	Website	Phone Number
BOMBAY Powai Mumbai 400 076	http://www.jee.iitb.ac.in	022- 25767062 25722601
DELHI Hauz Khas New Delhi	http://www.jee.iitd.ac.in	011- 26582002 26591735

110 016		
GUWAHATI		0361-
North	http://www.jee.iitg.ac.in	2690795
Guwahati		2690321-328
781 039		
KANPUR		0512-
Kanpur	http://www.jee.iitk.ac.in	2597236
208 016		2597335
KHARAGPUR		03222-
Kharagpur	http://www.jee.iitkgp.ac.in	288181
721 302		278241
MADRAS		044-
Chennai	http://www.jee.iitm.ac.in	22578098
600 036		22578095
ROORKEE		01332-
Roorkee	http://www.iitr.ac.in/jee	279805
247 667		279806

BRAINWAVE: *The only possible idea of India is a nation that is greater than the sum of its parts.*

KEEP IN MIND: *Emergence of India as a new major global player; similar to the rise of Germany in the 19th century and America in the 20th century; will transform the geopolitical landscape, with impacts potentially as dramatic as those of the previous two centuries.*

THINK ZONE: *In spite of the communal problems; the strange rise of India.*

20

Quest Questions

FREQUENTLY ASKED QUESTIONS

WHAT IS REQUIRED TO GET INTO IIT?

Strong will power, dedication, determination to win, focusing on the goal and lots of hard work is required to get in IIT.

HOW MANY HOURS DO I PUT IN THE CLASS XI? WHEN SHOULD I FINISH THE SYLLABUS OF IITJEE?

Study 5-6 hrs along with your school. Try to create your base right now, and try and do Calculus. Before the start of class XII preparation, enjoy reading new material, and learn new things.

WHAT TO PREPARE A DAY BEFORE JEE? IS THE JEE A TEST OF SPEED, ACCURACY OR CONCEPTUAL UNDERSTANDING?

Relax! Go for a walk for a couple of hours before the exam and just look over the list of formulae that you have prepared. JEE examination requires speed, accuracy, and more importantly conceptual understanding.

WHAT IS IQ? HOW IMPORTANT IS IQ?

IQ is a genetic given that cannot be changed by life experience, and that our destiny in life is largely fixed by these aptitudes. It stands for Intelligence Quotient. An IQ test shows the relationship between the child's mental growth and development, and his age. An IQ score of 90-110 is considered to be normal or average. A score of above 130 is considered above average. A score of above 140 is that of a genius. Very different levels of intelligence can be detrimental to a long-term relationship. A highly intelligent person's inclinations to protect, rescue, parent or 'improve' a much less intelligent partner, or to make him or herself feel better by comparison may later backfire in a relationship. Intelligence and level of education are not synonymous.

HOW IMPORTANT IS EQ (EMOTIONAL QUOTIENT) IN PREPARATION FOR IIT-JEE?

Unlike IQ, with its nearly one-hundred-year history of research with hundreds of thousands of people, EQ is a new concept. One has to be emotionally strong during preparations as well as at the time of examination because it is highly essential that the person should be able to answer everything that he had learnt. Anxiety or nervousness in such critical time will surely affect the results and to overcome such situations one had to build up enough confidence.

WHAT IS PERSONAL COUNSELLING? HOW DO I KNOW IF I NEED THE SERVICES OF A PROFESSIONAL COUNSELOR?

Counselling is a process through which a

collaborative, helping, and confidential relationship is formed between a counsellor and client in order to assist the client in better understanding him/herself. Clients are assisted in understanding their thoughts, feelings, and behaviours, and how they deal with various situations or relationships that they experience as problematic.

Some signs to watch for include feeling overwhelmed, helpless, and sad over a prolonged period of time. Even though you are trying to deal with your problems and have the assistance of family and friends, your problems do not seem to get better. You may find yourself feeling more irritable than usual, arguing more with those around you, withdrawing from social activities, friends, and family. You may not be attending classes regularly, completing assignments, or concentrating as well as you are accustomed to.

HOW TO ADDRESS THE TEACHER? HOW TO BE A GOOD STUDENT?

One subject with numerous misunderstandings is how we should address our teachers. The teacher is a figure of great importance. He is the person responsible for leading the students in the right direction, to progress and development. Students cherish the teacher, and their teacher loves the students in turn. The relationship between the teacher and his students is mutually caring and supporting.

A conscientious student has a definite plan for doing his/her assignments. A true student has a schedule for doing and completing all school work first, with no necessary breaks.

WHAT TO STUDY FOR TOMORROW'S PHYSICS EXAM?

By the time you read this answer, you will probably have sat your 'Transport' test! However, I shall give some general advice about studying. In a nutshell, you should study all of your notes, including all of the relationships. However, it is of little use trying to learn and write all of the relationships that you have been given. It is better to use the relationships by practicing as many examples as you can.

You will find examples in your notes, in your textbook, if you have one, and in last year's papers. The more you practise examples using all of the relationships, the more competent and confident in your ability you will become. One final point, learn the units of all quantities and don't forget to include the correct unit in the final answer to all your calculations.

HOW DO YOU COPE WITH THE STRESS OF MATHEMATICS EXAMS?

Most people get nervous about exams. That is not necessarily a bad thing. The important thing is to control your nerves and keep your head. You are more likely to be able to do this if you are well prepared for your exam. However remember that the examination also requires you to show that you can solve problems. This means that you may be faced with a situation, which is new to you. Don't panic when this happens. Read the question carefully. It is asking you to apply your knowledge of Mathematics and use it to solve a problem. You need a good knowledge base in order to be able to do Mathematics. If you do not know the formula, rules and relationships of Mathematics you will never be able to use them. So it all boils down to hard work.

WHAT ARE THE REVISION TECHNIQUES?

I would recommend don't take on too much at once. Pace yourself. Start now. Short regular sessions in the lead up to your examination are better than infrequent, lengthy cramming sessions. Practise questions are also to be included so that you can check up on the effectiveness of your revision. Make use of the revision material. Once you have revised a complete section, have a look at the questions on that section from last year's examination papers. That way you will get a feel for the standard that is expected of you. Ask yourself what is the question asking me to do? What does the examiner expect of me? Have I to calculate? Have I to describe? Have I to explain?

Write down the important rules and relationships that you are expected to be able to recall for the examination. Don't just learn them in parrot fashion. Discuss them with your friends. When you try to explain something to your friend, sometimes you find gaps in your own understanding. Don't be afraid to admit that you are having difficulty. Speak to your teacher. Help yourself!

IN PHYSICS THERE IS TOO MUCH TO LEARN. I AM UNABLE TO CONCENTRATE ON IT. PLEASE SUGGEST WAYS OF OVERCOMING THIS PROBLEM.

At first sight it does seem as though there is a lot to learn. But really there is not all that much to it. The important bits are the relationships and definitions. For example, you need to know what frequency, wavelength, speed, acceleration, force, current, and voltage etc. mean. You need to learn the definition of terms like these. There is no short cut. You have to sit down and study them. Then you have to know the relationships in which these terms are used. For example, force = mass x acceleration, resistance = voltage/current.

Divide your work into sections; tackle one section at a time. Slow and steady. This will help your confidence. Divide and you will conquer!

WILL IITJEE PREPARATION COVER OTHER ENGINEERING EXAMINATION TOO?

Yes, definitely.

BRAINWAVE: *Explore the world and experience the glory of nature, like a sensational sunset that fills your soul or a full moon set against a star-filled sky; realize your best through fulfilling work.*

KEEP IN MIND: *Among us who craft extraordinary careers and spectacular lives are those who spend most of their time giving their best out on the extra mile.*

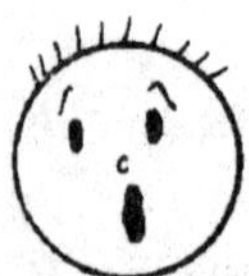

THINK ZONE: *Who dares nothing; need hope for nothing.*

About the Author

SUBHASH JAIN, M.Sc. (Physics) from the University of Rajasthan, is an experienced educator and teacher-trainer and an enthusiastic presenter. He has to his credit numerous workshops, training seminars, professional development program and consultations for educators and parents; spanning over the last two decades. He has also trained teachers of six senior secondary schools of NIMS, Dubai. Many of his papers and articles have been published in national and international newspapers, journals and magazines. His popular books, 'How to Excel in Examination' & 'Improve Your Memory' have been translated into various Indian languages.